PENGUIN

THE EPIC OF GILGAMESH

N. K. SANDARS studied, soon after the war, with Professor Gordon Childe at the Institute of Archaeology, University of London, and took the diploma of the Institute. She continued to work at Oxford, taking a B.Litt. degree in the prehistory of Europe, and thereafter she worked on the prehistory of the Aegean, receiving a studentship at St Hugh's College, Oxford, a scholarship from Oxford University and a travelling prize from the University of Liverpool. She has travelled extensively in Europe and in the Near and Middle East, and has taken part in excavations in the British Isles and overseas. She has contributed articles to various journals and is the author of *Bronze Age Cultures in France* (1957), *Prehistoric Art in Europe* (Pelican History of Art, 1968), *Poems of Heaven and Hell from Ancient Mesopotamia* (Penguin Classics, 1971) and *The Sea Peoples* (1978). She has written and lectured extensively on the poet and painter David Jones, and on the origins and history of art. N. K. Sandars is a fellow of the British Academy and of the Society of Antiquaries of London and a corresponding member of the German Archaeological Institute. A book of her poems, *Grandmother's Steps and Other Poems*, was published in 2000 by Poets' and Painters' Press.

THE EPIC OF GILGAMESH

AN ENGLISH VERSION WITH AN INTRODUCTION

BY

N. K. Sandars

*

REVISED EDITION INCORPORATING

NEW MATERIAL

PENGUIN BOOKS

PENGUIN BOOKS

Published by the Penguin Group
Penguin Books Ltd, 80 Strand, London WC2R 0RL, England
Penguin Putnam Inc., 375 Hudson Street, New York, New York 10014, USA
Penguin Books Australia Ltd, 250 Camberwell Road, Camberwell, Victoria 3124, Australia
Penguin Books Canada Ltd, 10 Alcorn Avenue, Toronto, Ontario, Canada M4V 3B2
Penguin Books India (P) Ltd, 11 Community Centre, Panchsheel Park, New Delhi – 110 017, India
Penguin Books (NZ) Ltd, Cnr Rosedale and Airborne Roads, Albany, Auckland, New Zealand
Penguin Books (South Africa) (Pty) Ltd, 24 Sturdee Avenue, Rosebank 2196, South Africa

Penguin Books Ltd, Registered Offices: 80 Strand, London WC2R 0RL, England

www.penguin.com

This translation first published 1960
Reprinted with revisions 1964
Reprinted with revisions 1972
60

Copyright © N. K. Sandars, 1960, 1964, 1972
All rights reserved

Printed in England by Clays Ltd, St Ives plc
Set in Monotype Bembo

ISBN-13: 978–0–140–44100–0

CONTENTS

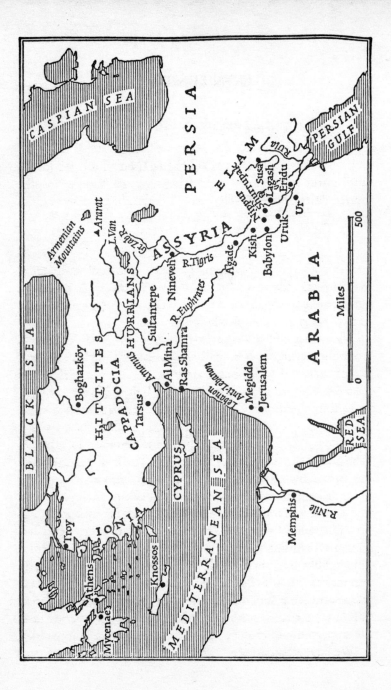

INTRODUCTION

1. *The History of the Epic*

THE Epic of Gilgamesh, the renowned king of Uruk in Meso-
potamia, comes from an age which had been wholly forgotten,
until in the last century archaeologists began uncovering the
buried cities of the Middle East. Till then the entire history of
the long period which separated Abraham from Noah was
contained in two of the most forbiddingly genealogical
chapters of the Book of Genesis. From these chapters only two
names survived in common parlance, those of the hunter
Nimrud and the tower of Babel; but in the cycle of poems
which are collected round the character of Gilgamesh we are
carried back into the middle of that age.

These poems have a right to a place in the world's literature,
not only because they antedate Homeric epic by at least one and
a half thousand years, but mainly because of the quality and
character of the story that they tell. It is a mixture of pure
adventure, of morality, and of tragedy. Through the action we
are shown a very human concern with mortality, the search for
knowledge, and for an escape from the common lot of man.
The gods, who do not die, cannot be tragic. If Gilgamesh is not
the first human hero, he is the first tragic hero of whom any-
thing is known. He is at once the most sympathetic to us, and
most typical of individual man in his search for life and under-
standing, and of this search the conclusion must be tragic. It is
perhaps surprising that anything so old as a story of the third
millennium B.C. should still have power to move, and still
attract readers in the twentieth century A.D., and yet it does.
The narrative is incomplete and may remain so; nevertheless
it is today the finest surviving epic poem from any period until
the appearance of Homer's *Iliad*: and it is immeasurably older.

We have good evidence that most of the Gilgamesh poems

were already written down in the first centuries of the second millennium B.C., and that they probably existed in much the same form many centuries earlier, while the final recension, and most complete edition, comes from the seventh century library of Assurbanipal, antiquary and last great king of the Assyrian Empire. This Assurbanipal was a formidable general, the plunderer of Egypt and Susa; but he was also the collector of a notable library of contemporary historical records, and of much older hymns, poems, and scientific and religious texts. He tells us that he sent out his servants to search the archives of the ancient seats of learning in Babylon, Uruk, and Nippur, and to copy and translate into the contemporary Akkadian Semitic those texts which were in the older Sumerian language of Mesopotamia. Amongst these texts, 'Written down according to the original and collated in the palace of Assurbanipal, King of the World, King of Assyria', was the poem which we call the Epic of Gilgamesh.

Not long after the completion of this task of collation the epic was virtually lost and the hero's name forgotten, or disguised and garbled out of recognition; until it was rediscovered in the last century. This discovery was due, in the first place, to the curiosity of two Englishmen, and thereafter to the labours of scholars in many different parts of the world, who have pieced together, copied, and translated the clay tablets on which the poem is written. It is a work which continues, and more gaps are being filled in each year; but the main body of the Assyrian Epic has not been altered in essentials since the monumental publications of text, transliteration, and commentary by Campbell Thompson in 1928 and 1930. More recently, however, a new stage has been reached and fresh interest aroused by the work of Professor Samuel Kramer of Pennsylvania, whose collection and translation of Sumerian texts have carried the history of the Epic back into the third millennium B.C. It is now possible to combine and compare a far larger and older body of writings than ever before.

2. *The Discovery of the Tablets*

The discovery of the tablets belongs to the heroic age of excavation in the mid nineteenth century, when, although methods were not always so scrupulous nor aims so strictly scientific as today, the difficulties and even dangers were greater, and results had an impact which profoundly altered the intellectual perspective of the age. In 1839 a young Englishman, Austen Henry Layard, set off with a friend on an overland journey to Ceylon; but in Mesopotamia he was delayed by a reconnaissance of Assyrian mounds. The delay of weeks was lengthened into years, but in time Nineveh and Nimrud were excavated; and it was from these excavations that Layard brought back to the British Museum a great part of the collection of Assyrian sculptures, along with thousands of broken tablets from the palace of Nineveh.

When Layard began excavating at Nineveh he hoped to find inscriptions, but the reality, a buried library and a lost literature, was more than he could have expected. In fact the extent and value of the discovery was not realized till later when the clay tablets with wedge-shaped characters were deciphered. Some, inevitably, were lost; but over twenty-five thousand broken tablets, a huge number, were brought back to the British Museum. The work of decipherment was begun by Henry Rawlinson, at the residency in Baghdad, where he was stationed as political agent. Before going to Baghdad, Rawlinson, then an army officer in the employ of the East India Company, had discovered what was to prove a principal key to the decipherment of cuneiform in the great inscription, the 'Record of Darius', on the rock of Behistun near Kermanshah in Persia, which is written with cuneiform (wedge-shaped) characters in the Old Persian, Elamite, and Babylonian languages. The work begun by Rawlinson in Baghdad was continued in the British Museum when he returned to England in 1855; and soon after his return he started publishing the *Cuneiform Inscriptions of*

Western Asia. In 1866 he was joined, as an assistant in the work on the tablets, by George Smith.

Meanwhile Rassam, Layard's collaborator and successor at Nineveh, had excavated in 1853 that part of the library in which were the tablets of the Assyrian collation of the Gilgamesh Epic. A realization of the importance of the discovery did not come till twenty years later, when in December of 1872, at a meeting of the newly founded Society of Biblical Archaeology, George Smith announced that 'A short time back I discovered among the Assyrian tablets in the British Museum an account of the flood.' This was the eleventh tablet of the Assyrian recension of the Epic of Gilgamesh. Soon after this first announcement Smith published the *Chaldean Account of the Deluge*, and with it the outline of the Gilgamesh narrative. Interest was immediate and widespread; but the Deluge tablet itself was incomplete, so the search for more tablets was renewed. The *Daily Telegraph* contributed 1,000 guineas towards further excavation at Nineveh, which George Smith was to undertake for the British Museum. Quite soon after his arrival at Nineveh, Smith found the missing lines from the description of the flood, which was then, as it still is today, the most complete and best preserved part of the whole Epic. Many more tablets were found in this and the following year, and Smith was able to fill in the broad outline of the Assyrian version before, in 1876, he succumbed to sickness and hunger, and died near Aleppo at the age of thirty-six; but already he had opened up a new field in Biblical studies and in ancient history.

When publishing the Assyrian 'Deluge' Smith had stated that this was evidently a copy from a much older version made at Uruk, the biblical Erech, known today as Warka. Some years earlier, between 1849 and 1852, W. K. Loftus, a member of the Turko-Persian Frontier Commission, had spent two short seasons digging at Warka, where he found puzzling remains, including what are now known to be third-millennium mosaic walls, and also tablets. But Warka had to wait for further attention till the twenties and thirties of this century, when the Germans carried out massive excavations which have revealed a long series of buildings, as well as sculptures and tablets. Thanks to this work a great deal is now known about early Uruk, its temples, and the life of its inhabitants.

Even more important for the history of the Gilgamesh Epic were the activities of an American expedition from the University of Pennsylvania, led by John Punnet Peters, which at the end of the nineteenth century started work on the mound of Niffar, ancient Nippur, in Southern Iraq. By this time considerably more experience had been gained of the problems connected with excavating ancient cities: but there were still many hazards. The first season at Nippur in 1888–9 began light-heartedly with the arrival of Peters and his party at the site in a wild gallop through the canebrakes on rearing stallions; but their last view of the mound at the end of the season was of hostile Arabs performing a war-dance on the ruins of the camp. Nevertheless the work continued the following year, and a total of from thirty to forty thousand tablets was found and distributed between museums in Philadelphia and Istanbul. These tablets include a small group on which are found the oldest versions of the Gilgamesh cycle in the Sumerian language. Work proceeds in the field and among museum archives. Recent additions have been made by the publication of tablets from Ur in the British Museum, and tablets have been identified in Baghdad and elsewhere, some historical, and some directly connected with the text. Division of the material has complicated the work of decipherment, for in some cases one half of an important tablet has been stored in America and the other in Istanbul, and copies of both must be brought together before the contents are understood.

The majority of ancient texts are commercial and administrative documents, business archives, lists, and inventories which though profoundly interesting to the historian, are not for general reading. The recent decipherment of the so-called 'linear B' script of Bronze Age Mycenae and Crete has revealed no literature. A huge library discovered at Kültepe in Central Anatolia is entirely made up of records of business transactions; and apart from a solitary text, and that a curse, there is not one of a literary kind. The importance of the excavations at Nippur, Nineveh, and other great centres of early civilization in Mesopotamia is that they have restored a literature of high quality and of unique character.

The Gilgamesh Epic must have been widely known in the second millennium B.C., for a version has been found in the archives of the Hittite imperial capital at Boghazköy in Anatolia, written in Semitic Akkadian; and it was also translated into the Indo-European Hittite, and the Hurrian languages. In southern Turkey parts have been found at Sultantepe; while a small but important fragment from Megiddo in Palestine points to the existence of a Canaanite or later Palestinian version, and so to the possibility that early Biblical authors were familiar with the story. The Palestinian fragment comes from the tablet which describes the death of Enkidu and is closest to the account already known from Boghazköy. Excavation at Ras Shamra, ancient Ugarit, on the Syrian coast has brought to life an independent epic literature of which the written versions mostly date from the later part of the second millennium, and which was also known in the Hittite capital; it includes a fragment from a flood narrative that probably stems from a version of the Gilgamesh flood. At this period therefore there was considerable overlapping and some mingling of the various literary traditions, including those of the Hittites themselves; and recently a case has been made out for the probable existence of a rather similar Aegean Mycenaean poetic tradition, elements from which would have survived the dark age, and reappeared in Homeric and later Greek poetry. The whole question of the date and nature of this undoubted Asiatic element in Greek myth and early poetry is still debatable and clouded with uncertainty.

Whether or not the fame of Gilgamesh of Uruk had reached
the Aegean – and the idea is attractive – there can be no doubt
that it was as great as that of any later hero. In time his name
became so much a household word that jokes and forgeries were
fathered on to it, as in a popular fraud that survives on eighth-
century B.C. tablets which perhaps themselves copy an older
text. This is a letter supposed to be written by Gilgamesh to
some other king, with commands that he should send improb-
able quantities of livestock and metals, along with gold and
precious stones for an amulet for Enkidu, which would weigh
no less than thirty pounds. The joke must have been well
received, for it survives in four copies, all from Sultantepe.
The text has been translated and published recently by Dr
Oliver Gurney.

3. *The Historical Background*

The excavation of sites and decipherment of texts has taught us
a great deal about the historical and the literary background of
the Epic. Although only the last version, that of Assurbanipal's
library, has survived as a relatively complete work, it appears
that all the most important elements of the story existed as
separate poems in the older Sumerian literature, and may have
been, indeed probably were, composed and recited long be-
fore they were written down. While no element of the story
can be later than the destruction of Nineveh in the seventh
century, a recurring situation typical of the third millennium is
discernible behind much of the action, and probably provided
its context. Behind this again the tradition reaches back into a
preliterate age on the borderline of legend and history, a little
later than the Deluge, when gods were replaced by mortals on
the thrones of the city-states. This was the age of the Archaic
Sumerian civilization.

The Sumerians were the first literate inhabitants of Meso-
potamia, and theirs is the language of the oldest tablets from

Nippur which relate to Gilgamesh. They had already irrigated
the country and filled it with their cities, before it was conquered
by Semitic tribes in the course of the third millennium. They
were themselves probably conquerors from the north and
east, who arrived during the fourth millennium. The influence
of this gifted people, shown in laws, language, and ideas, per-
sisted long after they had been conquered by their Semite
neighbours. It has been justly likened to the influence of Rome
on medieval Europe. Their language was still written, like
the Latin of the Middle Ages, centuries after they had lost their
political identity. It is therefore no anachronism to find the
early Gilgamesh texts still written in this 'learned' language,
although most of them date from the beginning of the second
millennium, after the Semitic conquest.

Excavation has shown that the Archaic Sumerian or Early
Dynastic civilization of the early third millennium follows
notable flood levels at several important sites: Shurrupak, Kish,
and Uruk among them. These levels close the last prehistoric
period, the Jemdet Nasr Period of the archaeologists; but there
is no proof of their being strictly contemporary. An earlier
disaster, identified by Sir Leonard Woolley at Ur, was of only
local extent, and archaeological evidence does not support any
single overwhelming catastrophe; nor was a disastrous flood
among the earliest of ancient Sumerian traditions. In later
Sumerian, as in Old Babylonian writings, flood and deluge are
sent by the gods, along with equally catastrophic visitations
of plague, drought and famine. Five cities are named as existing
before the Deluge, and to them 'Kingship was let down from
Heaven'. After the catastrophe 'Kingship once more des-
cended', and the city-states which then arose were often at war
with one another. The semi-historical 'Sumerian King-List',
composed at the beginning of the second millennium, shows
Kish as the first city to gain pre-eminence; but after a time Uruk
defeated Kish and took away this supremacy. These two states
were traditional rivals. In the King-List Gilgamesh is named as

fifth ruler of the first post-diluvian dynasty of Uruk (see below).

Because of their wealth the cities were great prizes, tempting to the wild Semitic tribes of Arabia, and to the warlike people of Elam to the east, and of the Persian highlands. Not long after the fall of the dynasty of Uruk, when the Semites had established themselves at Agade in the north, Sargon, their king, claimed that he had a standing army of 5,400 soldiers. Amongst the chief of his exploits was the destruction of the walls of Uruk. These had been a by-word. Men said 'Uruk of the strong walls', and Gilgamesh was traditionally the great builder.

In the Sumerian Early Dynastic age each city already had its temples of the gods. They were magnificent buildings decorated with reliefs and mosaics, and usually comprising a great court and an inner sanctuary, with sometimes, as at Uruk, a ziggurat behind. This was a holy mountain in miniature: an antechamber between heaven and earth where the gods could converse with men. So when Gilgamesh calls on the goddess Ninsun, his divine mother, she goes up to the roof of the temple to offer prayer and sacrifice to the great Sun God. The temples were served by a perpetual priesthood, in whose hands, at one time, was almost the whole wealth of the state, and amongst whom were the archivists and teachers, the scholars and mathematicians. In very early times the whole temporal power was theirs, as servants of the god whose estates they managed. Later a single individual became 'tenant-farmer' and caretaker, till 'Kingship descended from Heaven', power was secularized, and the royal dynasties, competitive and aggressive in aspect, arose in turn. The prestige of the temples remained, however, great.

One of the causes of the militarism of the third millennium was economic. The southern part of Mesopotamia as far as the Persian Gulf was, and is, a flat hot land of marsh and plain, very productive when drained, but, apart from the date-palm, altogether without timber and without metals. The demands of the rival cities on their neighbours in the surrounding highlands soon passed beyond the level of peaceful trade. Merchant colonies and distant trading posts were set up, but caravan communication was often broken, and raw materials were then fetched by force from reluctant tribes in Persia, Arabia, or Cappadocia. Here then the immemorial enmities of hill-tribe and plainsman were established; they provide the setting for a group of Sumerian poems which describe the troubled relations between Uruk and Aratta, a state in the eastern hills.

In the historical material we have nearly contemporary records of several expeditions, undertaken during the third millennium, by Sargon of Agade and Gudea of Lagash, to protect their merchant colonies and bring back timber for their buildings; nor were they certainly the first. Cedar came from the Amanus mountains in north Syria and south Turkey, and perhaps from the Lebanon and from south-east Persia. It is written of Sargon that he made a victorious campaign through the northern lands; and Dagon his god gave him the 'upper region' as far as the 'Cedar Forest' and the 'Silver Mountain'. The cedar forest in this case is certainly Amanus. Again when Gudea, the ruler of Lagash, wished to build a temple for the god Ningirsu, 'They brought from Susa, from Elam and the western lands copper for Gudea . . . they brought great willow logs and ebony logs, and Gudea made a path into the cedar mountain which nobody had entered before, he cut its cedars with great axes, cedar rafts like giant snakes were floating down the river from the cedar mountain, pine-rafts from the pine mountain. Into the quarries where no one had been, Gudea the priest of Ningirsu made a path, stones were delivered in large blocks, also bitumen in buckets and gypsum from the mountains of Magda, as many as boats bringing barley from the fields.' Behind the solid fleshly Gudea we may see the shadowy figure of Gilgamesh, a great builder of temples and cities, who ventured into strange forests and brought back precious cedar-wood.

4. The Literary Background

Five poems relating to Gilgamesh have survived from Sumer-
ian literature. Of these, two are used combined with later
material in this version of the Epic; they are 'Gilgamesh and
the Land of the Living', and fragments from the 'Death of
Gilgamesh' which are now known to be part of a much longer
text of at least 450 lines. This uses language much like that
of a lament for Ur-Nammu, an historical ruler of Ur who
lived around 2100 B.C., which incidentally names Gilgamesh.
Another poem concerning 'Gilgamesh and the Bull of Heaven'
lies behind the corresponding episodes in the Ninevite collation
describing the flouting and revenge of the Goddess Ishtar. A
large part of the Sumerian 'Gilgamesh, Enkidu and the Nether-
world' was translated almost word for word and appended to
the Assyrian Epic (Tablet XII), with no attempt at integration,
although it is incompatible with the events described earlier
(Tablet VII), and seems to provide an alternative to the 'Dream'
and 'Death of Enkidu' which are placed at the centre of the
Assyrian poem. 'Gilgamesh and Agga' like the 'Death of
Gilgamesh' is known only in Sumerian. It is a detached and not
very heroic tale of debate and mild warfare between the rival
states of Kish and Uruk. Its temper, though typical of some
Sumerian poetry, is too far removed from the rest of the
Gilgamesh material for its inclusion in a 'Gilgamesh Epic'.
It is not surprising if Assurbanipal's clerks and scholars rejected
it; though of course it may have been unknown to them.

The story of the Deluge did not form any part of the Gilga-
mesh cycle in Sumerian literature, but was an independent
poem with, in the rôle of Noah, a hero named Ziusudra, which
means 'he saw life'. There is also an Old Babylonian 'Deluge'
dating from the first half of the second millennium, in which the
hero is named Atrahasis. In this poem the flood is only the last
among a number of disasters sent to destroy mankind. The
first part is taken up with other matters, including the creation of

mankind. A fragment from Ugarit in Syria has already been mentioned. A late version of the Atrahasis poem was written down in the reign of Assurbanipal. It is not possible to say at what time the flood was drawn into the Gilgamesh cycle, since evidence is lacking from the Old Babylonian period. There has been much controversy on the question of the relationship between the Genesis flood and that of the Assyrian, Babylonian, and Sumerian writers. The opinion, at one time widely held, that the Genesis account was a late refinement on a story once current in all the cities of Babylonia, is not now so general; while the view that it derives directly from a very old and independent history has many supporters. There is no need to enter this difficult controversy in order to follow the account of the flood as it stands in the eleventh tablet of the Gilgamesh Epic. The decipherment of fresh texts may throw more light on the whole question; but at present the Genesis account is probably best seen against a background of many very ancient flood stories not necessarily relating to the same disaster, and with different protagonists, both human and divine. Not all the versions current in Mesopotamia and the Near East in the third millennium need have survived till today. The persistence and independence of different stories is shown by the fact that the hero in the third-century B.C. account, which in the last resort derives from a Greek-speaking priest of Babylon, Berossus, is given the name of Xisuthros or Sisuthros, which can only be the Sumerian Ziusudra, although that name has dropped out of the known Semitic versions.

Outside the Gilgamesh cycle two Sumerian poems have survived (as usual incomplete), which are concerned with one Enmerkar, a forerunner of Gilgamesh on the throne of Uruk; in the Sumerian King-List he is placed second after the flood. In the Enmerkar poems the king is in conflict with the lord of another state called Aratta, which lies eastwards, in the highlands of Persia. The cause of the quarrel is commercial, and appears to revolve round the barter of corn from Uruk against

precious metals, gold, silver, lapis lazuli, and probably building
stone from Aratta. Although heralds and champions are
employed, the action is even less heroic than that in 'Gilgamesh
and Agga'. As might be expected from the provenance of
the poem, Uruk is in each case successful against Aratta.

Lugulbanda also is the hero of two poems. He stands third
in the King-List and is sometimes referred to by Gilgamesh as
his semi-divine 'father'. He is a more interesting figure than
Enmerkar and, like Gilgamesh, he is a wanderer. In 'Lugulbanda
and Enmerkar' he is the liegeman and champion of the latter.
Like Gilgamesh too he crosses great mountains and the river
Kur (that is to say the underworld river), before he brings
Enmerkar relief from his enemies. In 'Lugulbanda and Mount
Hurrum' he is left for dead by his companions on another
mountain journey, this time to Aratta. By means of pious
sacrifices he gains the protection of the Sun God; and, again
like Gilgamesh, on his wanderings through the wilderness, he
eats the flesh of wild animals and uncultivated plants as though
he were a poor hunter. A reference to this episode seems to be
intended in our Epic when Gilgamesh is reminded by his
counsellors of the piety of Lugulbanda and exhorted to make
sacrifices to the sun and 'not to forget Lugulbanda'. It is possible
therefore that the later compilers drew upon this cycle as well
as that of the original Gilgamesh.

Sumerian epic was probably the creation of a proto-literate
phase of archaic Sumerian civilization at the beginning of the
third millennium; but it was not written down till centuries
later. According to one widely held view these Sumerians had
arrived in Mesopotamia some time before 3000 B.C. Here, in the
fertile plains, they inherited the prosperity of the settled inhabi-
tants who, being illiterate, are known only by their beauti-
ful pottery and by their settlements in villages of reed-huts and
sun-dried brick houses. According to an alternative view the
Sumerians were themselves the earliest cultivators in Meso-
potamia. However that may be, the world described in the

'epics' is very much that of the early and middle third millennium, before the unification of the pantheon at the end of the millennium (under the third dynasty of Ur), and before the standardization and formalism of the second millennium.

Of the early literary writings the Enmerkar poems, as they stand, are less heroic tales than argumentative contests and disputes. Not enough of the Lugulbanda cycle has yet been translated to judge how far it is heroic and epic in character. Most of the remaining Sumerian poems are either hymns and laments addressed to the gods, or are concerned with their attributes and activities. A number of 'epics', all more or less fragmentary, are known from the Old Babylonian and later periods, but the protagonists are usually gods and monsters. Gilgamesh is the one human character of heroic stature who has survived, though heroic fragments may be embedded in other material, as the 'Song of Deborah' is set in the Book of Judges.

5. *The Hero of the Epic*

Our enjoyment of the story is not seriously affected by whether or not there was a historical Gilgamesh; but scholars have in fact been able recently to establish beyond doubt that a man, a king, named Gilgamesh lived and reigned in Uruk at some time during the first half of the third millennium. Controversy is limited now to whether he lived around 2700 or some hundred or so years later. Names of the forerunners and contemporaries of Gilgamesh have been found written on bricks and vases; while two semi-historical documents, the 'Sumerian King-List' already referred to, and the so-called 'History of Tummul' give conflicting historical and genealogical evidence. According to the first, Gilgamesh is fifth in line from the founding of the first dynasty of Uruk (after the flood) and reigned 126 years, but his son reigned a mere thirty years, and thereafter kings lived and reigned an ordinary human term.

The Tummul document, also dating from the beginning of the second millennium, tells that Gilgamesh rebuilt the shrine of the goddess Ninlil in Nippur, following an earlier restoration by kings of Kish.

The various chronological ambiguities are of minor importance compared to the establishment of Gilgamesh as an historical person: a king who probably led a successful expedition to bring back timber from the forests of the north and who was certainly a great builder. The walls of Uruk were a by-word, but they were not yet of burnt brick; this is an anachronism possibly due to misunderstanding of an earlier text by later redactors.

Remembered was the superior quality of the 'plano-convex' bricks used in the construction of the fortifications. Excavations at Warka have shown the magnificence of the temple buildings even in the proto-literate period; but Gilgamesh was also remembered as a just judge, and later report made him, like Minos of Crete, a judge in the Underworld, one to whom prayers were addressed and who was invoked by incantation and ritual. One prayer begins, 'Gilgamesh, supreme king, judge of the Anunnaki'.

At the beginning of the poem the hero is described. He is two parts god and one part man, for his mother was a goddess like the mother of Achilles. From her he inherited great beauty, strength, and restlessness. From his father he inherited mortality. There are many strands in the story, but this is the tragedy: the conflict between the desires of the god and the destiny of the man. The mother of Gilgamesh was a comparatively obscure goddess who had a palace-temple in Uruk. His father in the King-List is rather mysteriously described as 'lillû', which may mean a 'fool' or a demon of the vampire kind, as well as being high-priest. Gilgamesh in the Sumerian version is 'the priest of Kullab', a part of Uruk, but in moments of stress he calls on Lugulbanda as 'father'. Lugulbanda reigned in Uruk second before Gilgamesh and third after the flood.

He was a guardian and protector of the city, and is called a god; he reigned 1200 years.

In a work which has existed for so long and been subjected to such frequent copying and reshaping, it is no use looking for precise historical events. I have suggested that the political situation in the third millennium provides the most likely setting for the action. More striking is the degree of spiritual unity found throughout the cycle, Sumerian, Old Babylonian and Assyrian alike, which derives from the character of the hero, and from a profoundly pessimistic attitude to human life and the world. This attitude is, at least in part, a consequence of the insecurity of life in Mesopotamia, and of those 'overtones of anxiety' which Henri Frankfort described as being due to 'a haunting fear that the unaccountable and turbulent powers may at any time bring disaster to human society'. In the character of Gilgamesh, from the beginning, we are aware of an over-riding preoccupation with fame, reputation, and the revolt of mortal man against the laws of separation and death. The conflict between savage or 'natural' man in the character of Enkidu, and civilized man represented by Gilgamesh, seems less fundamental, though it has been re-emphasized by at least one recent writer.

The story is divided into episodes: a meeting of friends, a forest journey, the flouting of a fickle goddess, the death of the companion, and the search for ancestral wisdom and immortality: and through them all runs a single idea, like the refrain of the medieval poet, '*Timor mortis conturbat me*'. In the episode of the Cedar Forest it is only a spur on the hero's ambition to leave an enduring name; but after the loss of the faithful companion it is more urgent, 'How can I rest when Enkidu whom I love is dust and I too shall die and be laid in the earth for ever?' At the end it turns to mockery with lost opportunity and wasted hopes; till the final scene of the hero's own death where human ambition is swallowed up and finds its fulfilment in ancient ritual.

The cause of the pervasive pessimism of Mesopotamian

thought lay partly in the precariousness of life in the city-states, dependent on vagaries of flood and drought and turbulent neighbours; dependent also on the character of the gods, who were the powers held responsible for such conditions. Since the gods play a considerable part in the Epic it may be well to give some account of these frightening and unpredictable beings. Their names and chief attributes are listed in the Glossary (p. 120), but the few who play a decisive part in the action require rather more detailed description. Their names will seem bizarre and unfamiliar to Western ears, and the topography of their world is superficially so odd that a rather fuller explanation seems necessary. The reader may, however, if he pleases, leave aside the following section until he wishes to know more about the chief gods and their habitations in the heavens or in the underworld.

6. The Principal Gods of the Epic

The cities of Mesopotamia shared a common pantheon, but the gods were not worshipped everywhere under the same names. The Semites when they invaded Mesopotamia inherited most of the Sumerian gods, but they altered their names, their mutual relations, and many of their attributes. It is not possible to say today if any were native to Mesopotamia, and belonged to the still older stratum of the population which may have been in occupation of the land before the arrival of the Sumerians, but throughout it is the known Sumerian gods who play the chief rôle in the Epic; and this is an additional argument, if any were needed, in favour of the great antiquity of all the episodes. Later gods such as Marduk of Babylon are never mentioned.

Each city had its own particular protector who looked after its fortunes and had his house within its walls. Anu (Sumerian An) was a father of gods, not so much Zeus as Uranus, the sky-god who to the Greeks was little more than an ancestral link in the chain of creation; from whose union with Earth, according to some of the genealogies, came Ocean, the rivers, the seas, the Titans and last of all, Cronos the father of Zeus. A reconstruction of the Sumerian theogony has been made by Professor Kramer, according to which An was the first-born of the primeval sea. He was the upper heavens, the firmament, not the air that blows over the earth. Like Uranus he was united to earth (Sumerian Ki) and begot Enlil, the god of the air. At this time the world was still in darkness and Enlil, the air, was imprisoned between the dark ceiling of heaven, a night sky without stars, and the earth's surface. So Enlil begot the moon Nanna (Semitic Sin), who travelled in a boat bringing light to the lapis lazuli heavens; and Nanna in turn begot the sun Utu (Semitic Shamash), and Inanna (Semitic Ishtar) goddess of love and war. The texts are still very obscure; one of them forms the introduction to the Sumerian poem of the descent of Enkidu to the underworld. Anu is not yet so detached as the Greek Uranus, but neither is he any more the active creator of gods. This supreme position was gradually usurped by Enlil, and in our poem it is Enlil who pronounces destinies in sign of authority. But he in turn was to fall before the newcomer, Babylonian Marduk.

Enlil, whose city was Nippur, was the storm and wind, breath and 'the word' of Anu; for according to the hymns in his praise, 'The spirit of the word is Enlil, the spirit of the heart of Anu.' This Enlil is power in action, where Anu is power in being. He is 'the word which stilleth the heaven above', but he is also 'a rushing deluge that troubles the faces of men, a torrent which destroys the bulwarks'. In the Gilgamesh Epic he appears oftenest in his destructive aspect; and beside him Anu is a remote being who lives far away in the firmament, beyond the gate of heaven. In one text he seems to encourage the journey to the Cedar Mountain, but it is also he who rebukes Gilgamesh and Enkidu for killing its guardian.

Equally important in the Epic are the kindly and just Sun God Shamash, whom the Sumerians called Utu, and Ishtar the

beautiful but also terrible goddess of love. The sun is still
'shams' in Arabic, and in those days Shamash was the omni-
scient all-seeing one, the great judge to whom anxious mortals
could make their appeal against injustice, and know that they
were heard. The hymns from Nineveh describe his many
attributes: 'All mankind rejoice in you, O Shamash, all the
world longs for your light . . . in a hollow voice feeble man
calls out to you . . . when his family is far away and his city
far-off, the shepherd boy fearful of the open field comes before
you, the shepherd in confusion among his enemies . . . the
caravan which marches in dread, the trader, the pedlar with
his bag of weights.' Nothing escapes the sun's eye, 'Guide and
beacon who constantly passes over the infinite seas, whose
depths the great gods of heaven do not know; your gleaming
rays go down into the Pit, and the monsters of the deep see
your light . . . you make it to burn over unknown stretches of
distance for countless hours . . . by your terrible brilliance the
land is overwhelmed.' The two aspects of the god as omni-
science and justice are united in the figure of the net: 'Spread
out is your net to catch the man who covets', and 'Thrown
down like a net over the land are your rays.' He is also the god
of oracles: 'By the cup of the diviner, by the bundle of cedar-
wood, you teach the priest of the oracle, the interpreter of
dreams, the sorcerer . . .'; and in another hymn he is the judge,
'Daily you determine the decisions of heaven and earth; at your
coming in a flame and fire all the stars of heaven are covered
over.' It was he also who gave to Hammurabi his system of
laws.

Ishtar (Sumerian Inanna) was worshipped in the great temple
in Uruk, together with Anu. She is the queen of heaven, and
as goddess of love and of war an equivocal character; 'an awful
and lovely goddess' like Aphrodite. Most of the gods had both
a benign and a dangerous aspect, even Shamash could be
terrible; but in this poem, except for a single moment, we see
Ishtar only in her darker character. That she could be gracious

is shown by a hymn of about 1600 B.C. 'Reverence the queen of women, the greatest of all the gods; she is clothed with delight and with love, she is full of ardour, enchantment, and voluptuous joy, in her lips she is sweet, in her mouth is Life, when she is present felicity is greatest; how glorious she looks, the veils thrown over her head, her lovely form, her brilliant eyes.' This is the radiant goddess of love as she first appeared to Gilgamesh, but her aspect very soon altered to become that of the familiar 'lady of sorrows and of battles'. In this character she is addressed in a hymn from Babylon: 'Oh, star of lamentation, brothers at peace together you cause to fight one another, and yet you give constant friendship. Mighty one, lady of battles who overturns mountains.'

The only remaining god to play an important part in the poem is Ea (Sumerian Enki), the god of wisdom, whose particular element was the sweet waters bringing life to the land, and whose house was at Eridu, which was then on the Persian Gulf. He appears as a benign being, a peace-maker, but not always a reliable friend, for, like so many exponents of primitive wisdom, he enjoyed tricks and subterfuges and on occasion was not devoid of malice. But here he acts as the great 'lord of wisdom who lives in the deep'. His origins are obscure, but he is sometimes called the son of Anu, 'Begotten in his own image . . . of broad understanding and mighty strength.' He was also in a particular degree the creator and benefactor of mankind.

Over against heaven and its gods lies the underworld with its sombre deities. In the old Sumerian myth of creation, already referred to, after An had carried off the heavens and taken possession of the firmament and after Enlil had carried off the earth, then Ereshkigal was borne away by the Underworld for its prize (or perhaps was given the underworld for her prize). The meaning of the myth is obscure, but this part of it seems to describe another rape of Persephone. Ereshkigal was sometimes called the elder sister of Ishtar, and possibly herself once a sky-goddess who became the queen of the underworld; but for her there was no spring-time return to earth.

The Sumerian name for the underworld, 'Kur', also meant mountain and foreign land, and there is often considerable ambiguity in its use. The underworld was beneath the earth's surface but above the nether waters, the great abyss. The way to it was 'into the mountain', but there were many circumlocutions for the place itself and for the way down. It was 'the road of the chariot' and 'the road of no-return'; nor are we ourselves so unlike the Sumerians in this respect, as can be proved by comparing the relative length of the entries under 'Life' and 'Death' in the English Thesaurus.

Later on, the old story of the rape (if such it was) seems to have been forgotten or to have lost its importance, and with it was lost the personality of 'Kur'; for, as with Hades, the grim god became little more than a dark place, while Ereshkigal is given other husbands. The Queen of the Underworld is an altogether terrifying being who is never more than obliquely described: 'She who rests, she who rests, the mother of Ninazu, her holy shoulders are not covered with garments, her breast is not covered with linen.' There are several poems, both Sumerian and Semitic, that describe the underworld. Sometimes it is the scene of a journey taken by a goddess or a mortal. A certain Assyrian prince, under the pseudonym of 'Kummu', has left a horrifying vision of death and the hereafter. It is a dark apocalypse in which the angels are all demons; where we recognize the sphinx, the lion and the eagle-griffin, the cherub with human hands and feet, along with many monsters of the imagination which haunted men's minds then and long after. They reappear continually on sealstones and ivories and carved rock-faces; and they have survived through the medium of medieval religious iconography and in heraldry into the modern world. If they have lost their power as symbols, the mysteries they represented are still the same as puzzle us today.

Throughout the narrative of the adventures of Gilgamesh

the presence of the underworld can be felt. It is the foreseen end of his journey however much he struggles to escape it, for 'only the gods live for ever'. It appears to Enkidu in a dream before his death, and in a separate poem the same Enkidu goes alive down the 'road of no-return' to bring back a lost treasure. But unlike the journey of the Greek heroes Heracles and Theseus when sent on similar errands, this journey was fatal; only a brief return was permitted, perhaps as a ghost with no more substance than a puff of wind which, when questioned by Gilgamesh, answered, 'Sit down and weep, my body which once you used to touch and made your heart's delight, vermin devour like an old coat.'

It would be an over-simplification to say that where the Egyptians give us the vision of heaven, the Babylonians give the vision of hell; yet there is some truth in it. The gods alone inhabit heaven in the Sumerian and Babylonian universe. Among mortals only one was translated to live for ever 'in the distance at the mouth of the rivers', and he, like Enoch who 'walked with God, and he was not, for God took him', lived in the dim past before the flood. Ordinary mortals must go to 'The house where they sit in darkness, where dust is their food and clay their meat, they are clothed like birds with wings for garments, over bolt and door lie dust and silence.' It is a depressing vision of heavy moping voiceless birds with draggled feathers crouching in the dirt. In this underworld there also lived the Anunnaki, the nameless 'Great Ones' who once, like Ereshkigal, lived above with the host of heaven, but who through some misdeed were banished to be judges of the underworld, much as Zeus banished the Titans, or like the fallen Lucifer. In Babylonia the soul of a dead man was exorcized with the incantation: 'Let him go to the setting sun, let him be entrusted to Nedu, the chief gatekeeper of the underworld, that Nedu may keep strong watch over him, may his key close the lock.'

The scene may not always have been so dark. There is one

Sumerian fragment which says that a righteous soul shall not
die and hints at a judge whom the virtuous need not fear: but
for the purposes of the Gilgamesh poems the underworld is
that place of wailing which Enkidu or his spirit describes in the
twelfth tablet. The journey there recalls the last book of the
Odyssey, when Penelope's suitors are led away, 'gibbering like
bats that squeak and flutter in the depths of some mysterious
cave when one of them has fallen from the rocky roof, losing
his hold on his clustered friends. With such shrill discord the
company set out in Hermes' charge, following the Deliverer
down the dark paths of decay. Past Ocean Stream, past the
White Rock, past the Gates of the Sun and the region of dreams
they went, and before long they reached the meadow of
asphodel, which is the dwelling-place of souls, the disembodied
wraiths of men.' Except for the 'Deliverer' Hermes, who takes
the place of the frightful being with talons and a sombre
countenance who led Enkidu away to the palace of Ereshkigal,
this is recognizably akin to the Babylonian vision of last things,
while even the simile of the bats was used by the writer of a
poem in honour of Inanna. It seems that the conception of such
a region of the dead was also familiar to the author of Psalm
XLIX when he wrote, 'They are appointed as a flock for
Sheol: Death shall be their shepherd: and the upright shall
have dominion over them in the morning: and their beauty
shall be for Sheol to consume, that there be no habitation
for it.'

The dying Egyptian, on the other hand, had a reasonable hope
of paradise to comfort and encourage him at the end. After
judgement and weighing of souls the righteous man could
expect, through a form of rebirth, to enter the fields of paradise,
'I know the field of reeds of Re . . . the height of its barley . . .
the dwellers of the horizon reap it beside the Eastern Souls.'
This rebirth was not for some single exceptional man alone,
nor the king alone, but for 'millions of millions . . . there is not
one who fails to reach that place . . . as for the duration of life

upon earth, it is a sort of dream; they say "Welcome, safe and sound" to him who reaches the West'.

7. *The Story*

Although the gods play a great part in the Epic, in its later form at least, *Gilgamesh* appears to have been as much a secular poem as the *Odyssey*. There is no suggestion that it was recited as part of religious ritual, as was the great Babylonian poem of Creation, the *Enuma Elish*, though it contains quasi-religious material in the laments over the dead, and in the set pieces of 'Wisdom'. It is a secular narrative, divided into loosely connected episodes covering the most important events in the life of the hero.

These poems give to Gilgamesh no marvellous birth and childhood legends, like those of the heroes of folk-lore. When the story begins he is in mature manhood, and superior to all other men in beauty and strength and the unsatisfied cravings of his half-divine nature, for which he can find no worthy match in love or in war; while his daemonic energy is wearing his subjects out. They are forced to call in the help of the gods, and the first episode describes how they provide a companion and foil. This was Enkidu, the 'natural man', reared with wild animals, and as swift as the gazelle. In time Enkidu was seduced by a harlot from the city, and with the loss of innocence an irrevocable step was taken towards taming the wild man. The animals now rejected him, and he was led on by stages, learning to wear clothes, eat human food, herd sheep, and make war on the wolf and lion, until at length he reached the great civilized city of Uruk. He does not look back again to his old free life until he lies on his death-bed, when a pang of regret catches hold of him and he curses all the educators. This is the 'Fall' in reverse, a *felix culpa* shorn of tragic development; but it is also an allegory of the stages by which mankind reaches civilization, going from savagery to pastoralism and at last to the life of the city. It has even been claimed from the evidence of this story that the Babylonians were social evolutionists! Recently Professor G. S. Kirk has made an interesting attempt to interpret Enkidu, his birth, his seduction and the fight with Gilgamesh, along lines of Levi-Straussian structuralism; with Enkidu representing 'nature' opposed to Gilgamesh as 'culture', the purpose of the story being to mediate the contradictions and so to resolve tension. While this may be one of the threads in the story, I do not think it is the most important. It implies a baseless identification of civilized man with disease and natural man with health and well-being; while to equate the literate and sophisticated milieu of second millennium Babylonia, and early first millennium Assyria, with the simple world of Homer's or Hesiod's Greek contemporaries, let alone that of Levi-Strauss's Amerindians, is highly misleading. It seems, in any case, that Enkidu is far from being a mere 'type figure'. Professor Gadd, introducing the latest translated fragments from Ur, has drawn attention to the conversation between the doomed and dying Enkidu and the Sun God, in which it is implied that he had been living happily in the plains with his wife 'a mother of seven'. Professor Gadd sees in his story a threefold tragedy: that of the husband seduced by meretricious charms to take up a life of which he soon tires, that of the nomad taken to the city and lost in it, and lastly the 'noble savage' tempted by a woman and winning through her a knowledge that brings him only unhappiness.

The great friendship between Gilgamesh and Enkidu that begins with a wrestling bout in Uruk is the link that connects all the episodes of the story. Even in a dream, before he had seen Enkidu, Gilgamesh was drawn to him by an attraction 'like the love of woman'. After the meeting Enkidu becomes 'a younger brother'; a 'dear friend', though in the Sumerian poems, in which there is no early history of Enkidu, the master and servant relationship is stressed to a greater degree. It is Enkidu who brings news of the mysterious cedar forest and its

monstrous guardian, the encounter with whom is the subject
of the second episode.

The journey to the forest and the ensuing battle can be read
on different planes of reality, like medieval allegory. The forest
is an actual forest, sometimes the Amanus in north Syria, or
perhaps in Elam in south-west Persia; but it is also the home
of uncanny powers and the scene of strange adventures like
those of Celtic heroes and medieval knights; and it is the dark
forest of the soul. On the first level, the historical, the need
of the cities for timber is the motive for the whole expedition.
Gilgamesh, the young king of Uruk, wishes to display his
power and ambition by building great walls and temples, as
did Sargon of Agade and Gudea of Lagash. But strange tribes
lived in the mountains who would resist any attempt at remov-
ing the cedars by force. There must be fighting before the valu-
able commodity can be shipped away, and in battle the gods of
the forest tribes would fight behind their own people: therefore
it was essential to enlist against them some one of the great
Mesopotamian gods, and use his stronger magic against their
magic. Shamash is won over with promises of a new temple to
be built in his honour, and he gives his special protection to the
enterprise. Among the terrors of the mountains were earth-
quake and volcano. A geological fault runs across Anatolia and
through Armenia, and volcanoes may still have been active as
late as the third millennium B.C., a fact which adds interest to
the accurate description of a volcano in eruption which is
contained in one of the dreams which comes to Gilgamesh on
the Cedar Mountain.

On the second level this episode is an adventure. Two young
heroes set out to win fame; the mountains and the cedars, with
their guardian, are the challenge beyond the horizon of the
everyday world. They go armed but alone, and alone they meet
the giant Humbaba, who has been variously identified as a
North-Syrian, Anatolian or Elamite god, according as to
whether the journey is visualized as leading to the northern or

the eastern mountains. He protects the forest with various enchantments; though the enchanted gate which Enkidu is supposed to open, to his hurt, may be a misunderstanding. When it reappears later, in his death-bed conversation, it is a gate in Uruk that is meant, the wood of which has come from the forest. Then there is a mysterious sleep which overcomes Gilgamesh as soon as he has felled the great cedar; and when at last Humbaba is tracked down in the deepest part of the forest, he almost overwhelms Gilgamesh with his 'nod' and the 'eye' of death. He is only subdued with the help of Shamash and the eight winds. These are a very potent weapon, for it was with the winds that the god Marduk overcame the primeval waters of chaos in the battle at the beginning of the world, as told in the *Enuma Elish*.

There is a third level also, for Humbaba is 'Evil'. The first time he is referred to it is simply this, 'Because of the evil that is in the land, we will go to the forest and destroy the evil'; so Gilgamesh plays the part of the knight who kills the dragon. Although in the conflict the two companions triumph, because they have taken sides amongst the gods using the weapons of Shamash to destroy the protégé of Enlil, they have incurred the anger of the quick-tempered, rancorous storm-god, and for this they will suffer later. In one view, indeed, the whole forest episode is a cruel trap set by Enlil in order to destroy Gilgamesh and Enkidu.

The forest is 'the Country of the Living', or simply 'the Country', lying somewhere on the outer bounds of earth and reality. In the middle of it is the mountain, which is both a seat of the gods and the underworld, the sender of dreams. But the forest is also related to that 'Garden of the Sun' which Gilgamesh will enter on a later journey, to meet again the great sun god, not in a dream, but face to face, for 'the Country belonged to Shamash'. The forest is oddly familiar, so is its guardian. 'Thou shalt see a vale like a great water-way and in the middle of the vale thou shalt see a great tree with the tips of its branches

33

greener than the greenest fir-trees. And under the tree is a fountain.' So Cynon is directed by the keeper of the forest in his wanderings, 'through the world and its wilderness' as told in the late Welsh romance from the *Mabinogion*. There he found 'the fairest vale in the world, and trees of equal height in it, and there was a river flowing through the vale and a path alongside the river'. Although this is twelfth-century Welsh it describes what Gilgamesh and Enkidu saw when they entered the cedar forest in almost the same phrases: the cedar in front of the mountain, the glade green with brushwood, and the broad way where the going was good.

The guardian of the forest in the romance had power over animals, which grazed around him in the glade, and the guardian of the cedar forest in the Semitic poem could 'hear the heifer when she stirred at sixty leagues distance'. This Humbaba is the perennial Monster Herdsman, like the ugly man with a club whom Cynon met or the Green Knight of the northern romance; he is a divinity of wild nature who would not alter through centuries any more than the forests themselves; but in the Sumerian poem he has a fiery aspect as well, perhaps connected with the volcano.

After what appeared to be a successful conclusion of the forest episode there comes a great act of glorification of Gilgamesh the King: robed, crowned, and in almost divine beauty, like Odysseus after his ordeal with the waves when Athene gave to him godlike beauty. At this moment the goddess Ishtar sees and desires him in love; she tries to woo him with tempting promises, after which comes a remarkable passage: the taunting of the goddess by a disdainful mortal. There is something here of Anchises, the herd-boy on Mount Ida, who in the Homeric Hymn was wooed by Aphrodite to his hurt, for 'He who lies with a deathless goddess is no hale man afterwards', or proud Hippolytus, or Picus and Circe in Ovid. So Ishtar is accused by the memory of her unfortunate lovers who survived miserably, one as a bird with a broken wing, another a wolf or a blind mole;

for this Ishtar has the power of Circe, and these seem like fragments from some once popular Babylonian 'Metamorphoses'.

Next follows the killing of the 'Bull of Heaven', a monster that personifies the seven years' drought which was sent by the angry goddess in punishment for her rejection by Gilgamesh. Anu at first refuses to create the bull, but when Ishtar threatens to break in the doors of hell and bring up the dead to eat with the living, he acquiesces, for this is not an idle threat, but was actually accomplished, as told in another poem. The acrobatic feat by which the bull was killed is like that performed in the bull games of Crete.

It is through *hubris* that disaster comes. Enkidu refused the prayer of Humbaba for mercy, and he insulted Ishtar. Gilgamesh seems less guilty; he was moved by Humbaba's prayer, though when they had killed the bull and the young men and singing girls crowded round to admire him, he let them cry, 'Gilgamesh is most glorious of the heroes, Gilgamesh is most eminent among men.' So retribution falls first on Enkidu. He is warned by a dream. He sees the gods in council and we hear the ominous question ringing out, 'Why do the great gods sit in council together?' Anu pronounces impartially, as is fitting in so lofty and remote a person: 'One of the two must die.' Shamash comes to defend them, but the quarrel between Shamash and Enlil, as though between sun and storm, breaks out again, and Shamash can only save one, Gilgamesh, his special protégé: Enkidu must die. In the night Enkidu has a vision of death which is one of the main sources for our knowledge of the Babylonian after-life. Another is contained in the independent Sumerian poem 'Enkidu and the Netherworld' and its Akkadian translation appended to the Gilgamesh Epic as Tablet XII of the Ninevite recension. Enkidu goes down alive into the Underworld in order to bring back a mysterious and perhaps shamanistic drum and drumstick that Gilgamesh has let fall into it. In spite of warnings he breaks all the taboos and is held fast, 'for the Underworld seized him'; but a hole is made in the earth's crust so that he (or his spirit) may return and describe what he has seen.

With the death of Enkidu more than half the story has been told. The companionship is broken and Gilgamesh is left alone; after having known the joy of an almost perfect friendship, he must learn to live without it; but this is more than he can bear. The knowledge that death is inevitable had earlier proved a challenge to bold undertakings and to victorious action; but now it stultifies action and brings the new experience of defeat. The great king is after all an ordinary mortal. In this crisis he thinks of his forefathers, and in particular of Utnapishtim, who, it was rumoured, found everlasting life, having entered the company of the gods. He was the survivor of the flood, another Noah, whom the gods took 'to live at the mouth of the rivers', and he is called 'the Faraway'. Then follows the search for ancestral wisdom which takes Gilgamesh to the limits of the earth, as did Odysseus's journey to find Teiresias. This second journey is not a repetition of the other to the Cedar Mountain. It can be based on no historical event; the topography is other-worldly in a manner which before it was not. The planes of romantic and of spiritual adventure have coalesced. Although clothed in the appearances of primitive geography it is a spiritual landscape as much as Dante's Dark Wood, Mountain, and Pit. As far as is known at present there is no Sumerian counterpart to this episode, unless it is to be found in the un-published Lugulbanda cycle.

After long wanderings through the wilderness, living like a poor hunter and wearing the skins of animals, Gilgamesh arrives at the mountain passes where he kills lions which he sees playing in the moonlight. This short episode is introduced almost casually, but it probably had a significance which is lost to us now, for on a great number of seals a figure, generally supposed to be that of Gilgamesh, is shown in combat with lions; and for the rest of the journey, until he reaches the Fountain of Youth, he wears the lion's pelt. The heraldic group of a warrior flanked by two lions rampant has passed into the iconography of the classical, medieval, and modern worlds, and is called even now 'the Gilgamesh motif'. We know that the lion which met Dante on the mountain's lower slope, 'Head held aloft and hunger mad', was the sin of Pride, while the panther carved on a medieval choir-stall may be the symbol of Christ, seen as the panther that killed a dragon, slept for three days, and then sweetened the world with its breath. But how should we understand these figures, which were commonplace to our Saxon and Medieval ancestors, without the researches of medievalists to explain them? It is not surprising that we have no clue now to the real significance of this lion combat. Only in the Hittite version there is a hint of some special connection between the lions and the Moon God.

From the pass where he killed the lions Gilgamesh came to the mountain of the sun with its awful guardians, part man, part dragon with a scorpion's tail. This description may be intended to remind us that the man-scorpion was one of the monsters created by chaos at the beginning of the world, according to the *Enuma Elish*. The mountain is shown on seals with the sun disappearing into it. It is the western horizon beyond whose ultimate range Shamash disappears at sundown and from which he returns at dawn; it is at the same time the wall of heaven and the gate of hell. The Sumerians thought of the sun as asleep through the night in the bosom of his mother earth, but the Semites held that he continued his journey in a boat, passing under the earth and over the waters of the underworld, till he came to the eastern mountain, to rise up in the morning with his bride the dawn. Gilgamesh in his journey through the mountain called Mashu retraces on foot the sun's journey; the twin peaks are both sunrise and sunset, and the goal at the end is the sun's garden by the shores of Ocean.

This garden of the gods is not the heavenly abode, but rather an earthly paradise, the country of the dawn 'Eastward in Eden'. But in contrast to the land of Dilmun, where the survivor of the flood was taken to live for ever, it is on this side of the waters of death. The episode survives, unfortunately, in a very fragmentary state, and the account of the wonders of the garden with its jewelled fruit is nearly lost; only enough remains to give us one of the rare hints of Eden-garden which survive in old Semitic. Here the sun walks in the early morning and sees Gilgamesh as an unkempt and desperate man; he remonstrates with him, but in spite of the god's warning that his quest is certain to fail, Gilgamesh is driven on. In a house beside the sea he finds the woman Siduri with her vineyards and wine-vats. She is also called *Sabit* which once meant 'barmaid' before it became a proper name. There may also be a connection between this name and that of the Chaldean Sibyl in Berossus. She is an enigmatic figure never explained, but her language is like that of Circe, herself a daughter of the sun, whose island home lay in the sea, where east and west were confused, and which grew magic herbs and moly. Like Circe and like her son Comus, Siduri dispenses the 'philosophy' of eat, drink, and be merry 'for this too is the lot of man'. The figure of the wine-bearer was still used by medieval Sūfī poets for whom it was the symbol of 'reality revealed'. From Siduri, Gilgamesh received instruction how to cross the waters of death, much as Odysseus had directions from Circe for the way to Hades, across the 'river of Ocean'. But Gilgamesh, unlike Odysseus, is alone and has no boat; he must find the ferryman, and the directions are doubtful. There is another great difference, for though it entails crossing Ocean and the waters of death, this is not an underworld journey, nor is the boatman Urshanabi a ferryman of the dead. It is still the journey the sun takes every night to 'the place of transit at the mouth of the rivers'. To reach Utnapishtim 'the Faraway', Gilgamesh must cross the same Ocean which was the last boundary of the known or knowable earth to all the ancients, Greeks, Semites, or Sumerians. It was an impassable barrier because it communicated with the waters of death and with the abyss, 'Absu', the waters that are above the firmament. Even sophisticated Romans were afraid of the Atlantic; and Caesar's crossing to Britain was considered an act of almost superhuman daring, because, unlike the Mediterranean Sea, the English Channel was the beginning of Ocean.

For the Sumerians, Ocean was somewhere out beyond the Persian Gulf, and there too was Dilmun, where the rivers ran into the sea, so that 'the mouth of the rivers' is exactly equivalent to the Greek 'springs of Ocean', there were the Elysian Fields and the blessed isles of Homer and Hesiod, 'towards night, in the far west in a soft meadow among spring flowers'. Like them, Dilmun was not for the ordinary dead. Utnapishtim did not die, but was singled out to live there for ever like Menelaus among Greek heroes, when he was sent to 'the Elysian plain at the world's end, to join red-haired Rhadamanthus in the land where living is made easiest for mankind, where no snow falls, no strong winds blow, and there is never any rain, but day after day the West Wind's tuneful breeze comes in from Ocean to refresh its folk'. There is a very old account of Dilmun, written on a tablet from Nippur. It describes how, when the world was young and the work of creation had only just begun, Dilmun was a place where 'the croak of the raven was not heard, the bird of death did not utter the cry of death, the lion did not devour, the wolf did not rend the lamb, the dove did not mourn, there was no widow, no sickness, no old age, no lamentation'.

That part of our texts which described the meeting of Gilgamesh with the boatman and their embarkation, in spite of recent publication of a little additional material, is still very defective. Certain seals show two figures, which may be Gilgamesh and Urshanabi, sailing in a boat with a serpent prow. This prow may explain the serpent which is referred to during the meeting between Gilgamesh and the Ferryman; but the nature of the 'Things of Stone', which Gilgamesh rashly smashes, remains mysterious and unexplained. All that can yet be said of them is that their destruction makes necessary the use of punting poles, and that they are connected in some way with 'wings' or 'winged beings or figures', but beyond this 'they retain for the present most of their secrets' as Professor Gadd, in a discussion of the new texts, wrote in 1966.

The encounter of Gilgamesh with Utnapishtim 'the Faraway' begins with one of those set pieces of 'Wisdom', all of which, like Siduri's exhortation to a life of carefree pleasure, while having a very pessimistic tone, seem intended to reconcile man to his lot on earth. It is followed by Utnapishtim's account of the flood. This is the best preserved of all the tablets in the Assyrian version, with over 300 extant lines. I have already referred to the older versions unconnected with Gilgamesh: the Sumerian 'Deluge', in which Ziusudra stands in the place of Noah or Utnapishtim, and the old Babylonian Atra-ḫasīs. There is a remarkable resemblance between the story told in Genesis and the Gilgamesh tablet, but there are also striking differences. In Genesis the city is not named, but in the other versions it is usually Shurrupak, the modern Fara, and one of the first of the Sumerian city-states to gain a pre-eminent position.

The account of the eleventh tablet begins with a council of gods. Such councils never boded any good for men and this is no exception. There is no explanation of the immediate cause of the gods' decision to destroy mankind. Probably it was much the same as in Genesis: 'The earth was corrupt before God, and the earth was full of violence', for later there is talk of 'laying his sin upon the sinner'. In the Sumerian story the account of the flood follows that of the creation of man, vegetation and animals, the institution of kingship and of the proper worship of the gods. Then unfortunately there is a long break in the text, which has obliterated the cause of the gods' wrath and their decision to destroy mankind by flood, It may be suggestive that the last decipherable phrase is connected with the cleaning and irrigation of small rivers. When the story does become intelligible the gods are divided much as in the eleventh tablet of Gilgamesh. Other flood stories were known in ancient Mesopotamia but the earliest Sumerian literary reference does not seem to be much older than the Old Babylonian Atra-ḫasīs of the early second millennium. In this poem the flood follows pestilence, famine and drought, each designed to exterminate mankind. In the definitive edition of W. G. Lambert and A. R. Millard these lines occur:

> Twelve hundred years had not yet passed
> When the land extended and the people multiplied,
> The land was bellowing like a bull,
> The god got disturbed with their uproar.
> Enlil heard their noise . . .

The description of the flood itself in Tablet III has so much in common with the language of Gilgamesh Tablet XI that it seems the latter must have been modelled upon it, or rather upon some lost Middle Babylonian recension.

In the Gilgamesh flood Ishtar and Enlil are as usual the advocates of destruction. Ishtar speaks, perhaps in her capacity as goddess of war, but Enlil prevails with his weapon of the storm. Only Ea, in superior wisdom, either was not present, or being present was silent, and with his usual cunning saw to it that at least one of the race of men should survive.

The dreadful havoc appalled even the gods; for Enlil summoned to his aid not only the horrors of the storm, but the Anunnaki, gods of the underworld, whose lightnings played about the rising waters. The description of the storm is more elaborate and impressive than the account in Genesis. In order to find language comparable to that which describes the black cloud coming from the horizon, which thundered within where the god of the storm was riding, it is necessary to go to the Psalms – '. . . darkness was under his feet. And he rode upon a cherub and did fly; yea, he did fly upon the wings of the wind. . . . At the brightness that was before him his thick clouds passed hailstones and coals of fire. The Lord also thundered in the heavens.'

In the Biblical story the same machinery is used: the building of the boat, the entry of the animals, the flood, loosing of the birds and the sacrifice; but while the god who 'remembered Noah' lives in awful isolation, in the Assyrian, as in the Sumerian stories, we are still in the world of factious, flustered, and fallible deities. There is real danger that the powers of chaos and destruction will get out of hand. Things do indeed go too far, and the gods are shocked by the results of their own action; but nothing shows more strikingly the difference in outlook and purpose than the conclusion. In place of God's solemn pledge to Noah, 'While the earth remaineth seedtime and harvest, and cold and heat, and summer and winter, and day and night shall not cease', there is the nauseating picture of gods swarming like flies over the sacrifice. Instead of the rainbow pledge, there is only Ishtar fingering her necklace and exclaiming that she will not 'forget these days'. But this is the word of the most notoriously faithless of all the gods. So, too, the immortality and semi-divine status which Utnapishtim, Atra-ḫasīs and Ziusudra win for themselves and their families is very different from the solemn covenant of the Bible, between God and a still entirely human Noah, through whom all mankind is given respite from anxiety. Part of the cause of the malaise present in the Mesopotamian psychology was this insecurity under which the people lived out their lives: the lack of a covenant.

The flood narrative is still an independent poem inserted into the framework of the Gilgamesh Epic. When it has been told we are back where we were; but it tends, like the other concluding incidents, to bring home to Gilgamesh the futility of his search. In spite of everything an obdurate hope remains with the hero; this must be crushed and shown for the evasion that it is. When challenged and put to the test Gilgamesh cannot even remain awake. At the Spring of Youth, where he receives the clothing which shows no sign of age, he experiences the irony of mere possessions outliving the body; while the plant of Youth Regained, brought with such difficulty from the sea's bottom, is briefly possessed and then lost; and so in this way the lesson is learnt for the last time. The text here is again very defective, but the snake that sloughs its skin needs no other gloss; it is the symbol of self-renewal. There is also a linguistic connection between the name given to the plant and that for bark of cassia which is called 'snake rind', that is to say, the sloughed snake-skin.

Why does Gilgamesh not eat the plant at once and so regain his youth? Is it because of an altruistic desire to share it with his people and give the old men back their youthful strength? Is this just another trick of the gods? I do not think it is, nor that Gilgamesh is continually cheated of an almost attained immortality; but rather that the purpose of each of these incidents is cumulative, and is aimed at breaking down his refusal to accept human destiny. Gilgamesh's search was not for any eternal renewal of nature, such as the goddess Ishtar might have given, nor for the mere escape from old age into a life of ease and idleness, such as Utnapishtim had been granted; but much more an earthly immortality with its opportunity for heroic action, and for glory on the earth like that of the gods in heaven. It needs the repetition of the lesson to drive home the truth that Gilgamesh, the king, is not different from other men. Only after the return of the snake to its pool does he at last accept the futility of struggling for what cannot be had, 'searching for the wind' as Siduri had said. The search is over, there is nothing more to do but go home.

The return is very summarily described and leaves much unexplained. It is like the breaking of a spell, when, at the end of trouble and search and with a prize almost won, everything suddenly returns to ordinary and we are back where we started, admiring the prosaic excellence of the city wall. All the fine things we had hoped to find – youth, eternal life, the dead friend – are lost. This ending has been described as 'Jeering, unsatisfying, without tragedy or sense of catharsis.' With this judgement I do not agree, for it is the true ending, it is what really happens, and in its way as tragic as the end of Hector under the walls of Troy.

The last act of all, the death of Gilgamesh, exists only in the Sumerian. It is a solemn lament; not so much a cry of individual sorrow, as part of a ritual, the elaborate burial of the dead. It is such a scene as the excavation of the Royal Cemetery at Ur has revealed with the mass immolations as well as the magnificent paraphernalia of the funeral: the gifts, banquets, robings, and the bread and the wine offered by the dead king to the gods of the underworld at his entry of the 'Land of No Return'.

8. Survival

This is the story which has survived precariously, to be rediscovered only within the last century; for when Nineveh fell in 612 B.C. to a combined army of Medes and Babylonians, the destruction that followed was so complete that it never rose again; and under the rubble of the Assyrian capital was buried the whole library of Assurbanipal. The Assyrians of the later Empire were not much loved by their neighbours, and the Hebrew prophet Nahum spoke no doubt for the sentiments of many when in 'The Burden of Nineveh' he exulted over its imminent fall: 'The chariots shall rage in the streets, they shall justle one against another in the broad ways: they shall seem like torches, they shall run like the lightnings. .... Nineveh is laid waste: who will bemoan her?'

This seventh century was perhaps the last point in the history of the Near East when a great literature, and a story like that of Gilgamesh of Uruk, could have so nearly disappeared. The flood narrative had become once more an independent story, but the mechanics, as told by Eusebius, quoting from Berossus in the third century B.C., have altered surprisingly little. In Babylonia the entire Epic probably survived rather longer than anywhere else, and copies are known from after the sack of

Nineveh; but survival was a matter of a particular pattern of
journeys and of adventures, which recurs in the frontierless,
timeless world of folk-tale and romance. Aelian, writing in
Greek c. A.D., 200 knew a Gilgamos, king of Babylon, and tells
a story of his birth not unlike that told of Perseus, and also of
Cyrus. Elements have been suspected in medieval Persian folk-
tales and even further afield; but it was a twilight survival.
Amongst the writings of the Near East and Mediterranean in
the classical age there is no direct awareness of our Epic.

One of the reasons for this disappearance may have been the
cuneiform characters in which it was written, and which were
passing out of use, soon to become unintelligible to the new
Mediterranean world. There may have been popular Aramaic
versions which have not survived, but the Persians, who
continued to use the old script, had their own literature and were
apparently very little sympathetic to the history and legends of
their late enemy. The Hebrews had still better reasons for
wishing to forget Assyria, Babylon, and all that concerned
them, except as a cautionary tale. Moreover, the century in
which Nineveh fell was the same that saw the emergence of the
modern poetic forms of the lyric and choral ode written in
alphabetic script. But if Greek lyric of the seventh century
is modern, the Greek Epic still belonged in part to the same
legendary world as Gilgamesh the king of ancient Uruk.
It would have been historically possible for the poet of the
Odyssey to hear the story of Gilgamesh, not garbled but direct,
for ships from Ionia and the Islands were already trading on the
Syrian coast. At Al Mina and at Tarsus the Greeks were in
contact with Assyrians. It is unlikely, but not impossible, that
Assurbanipal heard a Greek story-teller reciting the *Iliad* in
Nineveh.

It is possible that rather too much has been made recently of
the apparent similarities between early Greek and western
Asiatic mythology and legend. This is not the place to chase
those beguiling will-o'-the-wisps of criticism: whether Gilga-

45

mesh was a prototype of Odysseus or wielded the club of Heracles. It is less a case of prototypes and parentage than of similar atmosphere. The world inhabited by Greek bards and Assyrian scribes, in the eighth and seventh centuries, was small enough for there to have been some contact between them; and the trading voyages of Greek merchants and adventurers provide a likely setting for the exchange of stories; particularly if the ground had been prepared, centuries earlier, by Bronze-Age Mycenaeans in their contacts with the people of Syria, and possibly with the Hittites of Anatolia. Therefore it is not surprising that Gilgamesh, Enkidu, and Humbaba should seem to inhabit the same universe as the gods and mortals of the *Homeric Hymns*, Hesiod's *Theogony*, and the *Odyssey*. Common to all is the *mise-en-scène*, a world in which gods and demi-gods fraternize with men on a fragment of known earth which is surrounded by the unknown waters of Ocean and the Abyss. These men occasionally emerge from the penumbra of myth and magic as sympathetic, recognizable human beings, such as the Homeric heroes, and with them is Gilgamesh of Uruk.

When the Babylonian gods and their universe went underground it was only to reappear in later Mediterranean religions, and particularly in Gnostic beliefs; so too the heroes were transformed and survived, travelling westward as well as east. Gilgamesh has been recognized in the medieval Alexander, and some of his adventures may have been transferred to the romances. So perhaps behind the Welsh Cynon, behind Owen and Ivain, behind Sir Gawain searching for the Green Chapel through the northern winter forest with its oak trees and trailing moss, behind Dermot fighting the 'wild man' at the fountain (which is the way to the country under the waves) there is still the Sumerian Country of the Living, the Cedar Forest and the Silver Mountain, Amanus, Elam, Lebanon. These are stories of folklore and romance which run back from the medieval courts through Celtic legend and minstrelsy to archaic Sumer, and perhaps further, to the very beginning of

story-telling. Although the Sumerian hero is not an older
Odysseus, nor Heracles, nor Samson, nor Dermot, nor Gawain,
yet it is possible that none of these would be remembered
in the way he is if the story of Gilgamesh had never been
told.

Today ours is a world as violent and unpredictable as that of
Assurbanipal, the king of Assyria, the Great King, king of the
World, and of Nahum of Judea, and even of the historical
Gilgamesh, the king of Uruk, who made war and sent out
expeditions in the third millennium before Christ. The differ-
ence is only that for us the 'swirling stream of Ocean' lies not
over the rim of a flat horizon, but at the end of our telescopes,
in the darkness they cannot penetrate, where the eye and its
mechanical extensions turn back. Our world may be infinitely
larger, but it still ends in the abyss, the upper and nether waters
of our ignorance. For us the same demons lie in wait, 'the Devil
in the clock', and in the end we come back to the place from
which we set out, like Gilgamesh who 'went a long journey,
was weary, worn-out with labour, and returning engraved on
a stone the whole story'.

9. The Diction of the Epic

In works separated by as great a period of time as that which
lies between the Sumerian and the latest Semitic versions of the
Gilgamesh Epic there are naturally differences in diction as well
as feeling. The ancient writers themselves described the Epic
as 'the Gilgamesh Cycle', a poem in twelve songs or cantos of
about three hundred lines each, inscribed on separate tablets.
The Ninevite recension is written in loose rhythmic verse with
four beats to a line, while the Old Babylonian has a shorter line
with two beats. In spite of its primitive features of repetition and
stock epithet the language is not at all naïve or primitive; on the
contrary it is elaborately wrought. The short Homeric 'stock
epithet' is sparingly used; the Sun God is 'glorious' and Ninsun

is 'wise', but not invariably, and these epithets are far less frequent than those attached to a Hector or Odysseus. What we have in both the Sumerian and Semitic versions is the word for word repetition of fairly long passages of narrative or conversation, and of elaborate greeting formulae. These are familiar characteristics of oral poetry, tending to assist the task of the reciter, and also to give satisfaction to the audience. A demand for exact repetition of favourite and well-known passages is familiar to every nursery story-teller, along with the fierce disapproval of any deviation, however slight, from the words used when the story was told for the first time. Now, as then, an almost ritual exactitude is required of the reciter and story-teller.

We do not know how long the poem was recited, but the retention of those passages suggests an oral tradition alongside the written. They provide a special problem for the translator, particularly where they come very close together without narrative or emotional compulsion. This applies to the instructions to the hunter on his ruse for the capture of Enkidu, which are given in quick succession by his father, by Gilgamesh, and repeated by him himself. In this case I have compressed (perhaps a reciter would have filled out his material with interpolations). But in the case of the words with which Gilgamesh is greeted by the various characters whom he meets in his search for Utnapishtim, and his long replies, the effect is cumulative; each repetition enhances the sense of weariness, frustration, and obstinate endeavour, and must be retained; or again where repetitions in similar words, with slight variations, increase tension and lead to a climax, as in Gilgamesh's journey through the mountain. This, when spoken, would have left a powerful impression of time passing, and of the strain of the ordeal, so, though the effect is much diminished in reading, I have only slightly compressed. Indeed, how to express the passage of time appears to have been a considerable difficulty, and this device may have aimed at meeting it, for the same type of repetition occurs wherever a journey has to be described.

A number of the usual devices of poetic embellishment were used, including punning expressions, deliberate ambiguity (this in the Sumerian also), and irony. The simile does not appear often, but when it does it is with good effect. On the whole the descriptions are direct and vivid, like that of the volcano and the storm that precedes the flood. The 'poetry' is in the cast of mind which saw sheet lightning on the horizon as gods of the underworld raising their torches above their heads. The language of the Sumerian is different in quality, perhaps in part because it is closer to hymn and liturgy. The Akkadian lament over Enkidu is more elaborately expressed, but the Sumerian lament for Gilgamesh has a nobility and ritual force which the other lacks. We have become so used to the more sophisticated literary versions of myth, that we may be tempted to suspect a 'poetic' or 'literary' overtone where none exists, reading too much into symbols which chance to have caught the imagination of later and more self-conscious writers. How far a deliberate poetic effect was aimed at we cannot now tell, nor at what point freedom from ancient ritual sanctions may have been achieved. Once a myth has crystallized into literary form it is already dead as belief or ceremonial, but it is possible that, at least in the earliest strata of our material, this change was not yet complete, and for that reason we must not be surprised to find embedded in such early poems fragments of belief which appear grotesque or banal; while at other times we are confronted by the *disjecta membra* of a poetry which never quite emerges.

10. *Remarks on this Version*

This version of the Epic of Gilgamesh is not a fresh translation from the cuneiform. Such a translation would require a detailed knowledge of the languages in which the various parts have survived – Sumerian, Akkadian and Hittite are the principal – and is a task which I am not competent to undertake. Several scholarly translations into English, French, and German now exist, which provide accurate texts amplified by long explanatory notes. For the ordinary reader, who is not also an Assyriologist or student of Ancient literatures and history, these texts prove difficult reading, for they necessarily tend to emphasize rather than mitigate the short-comings of the original material. Every missing or doubtful word is marked by a gap or brackets; these are of different kinds according as to whether the word within the bracket has been supplied by the translator or by the ancient redactor. Moreover, the language is brought as close as possible to the structure of the Semitic or Sumerian original, which often makes poor English. Many happy exceptions exist and from these I have been able to benefit, as well as from the commentaries which explain the limitations and difficulties of various readings. This scholarly method gives the student and specialist what he needs, but presents the ordinary reader with a page which may look rather like an unfinished crossword puzzle. It has seemed, therefore, worth attempting a version which, while adding nothing that is not vouched for by scholarship nor omitting anything of which the meaning is beyond doubt, yet will avoid the somewhat uncouth appearance of the line by line translation and will give the reader a straightforward narrative.

I am well aware of the temerity of any such attempt and of the prime debt which I owe to the scholars who have made the translations out of cuneiform. I have been chiefly dependent on Alexander Heidel of the Oriental Institute, in the University of Chicago, for his *Gilgamesh Epic and Old Testament Parallels* (second edition 1949), and to E. A. Speiser for his translation, among other Akkadian texts, in the collection edited by J. B. Pritchard under the title *Ancient Near Eastern Texts Relating to the Old Testament* (second edition 1955; there is now a third edition, 1969, with supplementary material). All later translators have made extensive use of Campbell Thompson's translation (into English hexameters) and his commentary published in 1928 and 1930. For the Sumerian material I have used the translation of S. N. Kramer published in *Ancient Near Eastern Texts* and in his book *From the Tablets of Sumer*, 1956 (reissued in this country as *History begins at Sumer*, 1958). The important fragment from Sultantepe was published by O. R. Gurney in the *Journal of Cuneiform Studies* for 1964 and is found slightly modified in the second edition of *Ancient Near Eastern Texts*; other supplementary passages or variant readings are drawn from special articles in journals and will be referred to in their context below.

I have not followed other versions in giving the Epic in verse, believing that prose will provide a more direct and flexible means of communication, particularly in difficult passages, and for the same reason I have given up the division into tablets. Within the framework of the text there is still room for considerable variety of approach and interpretation, as a comparison of the different translations in existence soon shows. My aim throughout has been intelligibility, and as far as the surviving texts allow, a smooth and consistent story. Any version that aims at a unified narrative must be a collation. The 'Standard Text' created by the scribes of Assurbanipal in the seventh century was a collation, and so are all the modern versions. I have departed from the more usual practice by employing the Sumerian sources alongside the Akkadian and Hittite. This is not only because of their priority, and the fact that the Akkadian writers themselves drew on the Sumerian Cycle for the basis of most of the episodes in their Epic; but also because they fill important gaps, particularly in the 'Forest Journey', and they alone provide the 'Destiny' and the 'Death of Gilgamesh'. Moreover, their quality is very high.

The differences in detail between the Sumerian and the Old Babylonian are not greater than those that appear to exist between the Ninevite and Boghazköy recensions, which are generally combined by the modern translators; while the date of writing-down of the surviving Sumerian material (first half of the second millennium) is very close to that of the Old Babylonian of the Yale and Pennsylvania tablets (First Dynasty of Babylon). The Hittite version appears to diverge radically from the others in the later parts, but it is valuable at several points, particularly in the conflict with Humbaba (Huwawa) and the first meeting with Urshanabi.

The order of events is not always certain and is particularly confused in the Forest Episode; but the order of the episodes is fairly consistent. I have not followed the rearrangement of Tablets IV and V proposed by J. V. Kinnier Wilson (VII-Rencontre Assyriologique Internationale (1960), see below) according to which the dreams of Gilgamesh take place before his arrival at the forest. Although in some ways more logical, there are serious objections to this alteration. The sequence which I have followed is in the main that of Heidel and Speiser with their combination of Old Babylonian, Hittite, and Assyrian material, including the Sultantepe fragment. The use in addition of the Sumerian 'Gilgamesh and the Land of the Living' and the 'Death of Gilgamesh' has meant some modification of this arrangement. In the Forest Episode the Sumerian is sufficiently close to the other versions to be used directly to fill in the very defective description of the encounter with Humbaba. The chief point of difference is the Sumerian account of the 'fifty sons of the city' who accompany the two heroes on their journey, and whom I have omitted. A recently published Old Babylonian fragment relating to the fight against, and the killing of Humbaba provides a closer link with the Sumerian, and a recent Hittite tablet suggests yet another variant. In the preparations for the 'Forest Journey', the Sumerian, Old Babylonian, and Assyrian all give a slightly different sequence of events. I have used an amalgamation of the Old Babylonian and Assyrian versions except that, with the Sumerian, I have placed the appeal to the Sun God before the interviews with the citizens and the smiths.

The excuse for incorporating also the Sumerian 'Death of Gilgamesh' is that it makes a more satisfactory end than the conclusion of Assyrian Tablet XI. The reason for not using tablet twelve has already been given. It is incompatible with the account of Enkidu's death which we have already had, following the episode of the 'Bull of Heaven'. The Sumerian poem, of which this has been shown to be a literal translation, probably took the place of the dream and death of Enkidu described on the seventh tablet of the Ninevite recension. More open to possible objection may be my use at the beginning of the 'Forest Journey' of the Sumerian 'Destiny'. As Enkidu is the Interpreter of dreams on subsequent occasions, and since the Sumerian 'Destiny' came to Gilgamesh apparently in a dream, I have thought it permissible to insert it at this point, as well as repeating it at the end where, with the 'Death' (fragments 'A' and 'B'), it forms an appropriate tail-piece. Both the Old Babylonian and the Sumerian texts make Enlil the author of the 'Destiny'.

There are one or two other points that need explanation. I have omitted altogether Humbaba's hypothetical 'Watchman' at the Gate, because I think it is always Humbaba himself who is referred to. Though the language is ambiguous, a second watchman is not mentioned again and would be superfluous. The Old Babylonian fragment describing the killing of Humbaba I have used in full, after the Sumerian account, though they may really overlap. I have very slightly altered the sequence of lines at the beginning of the last journey (Assyrian Tablet IX); this is in order to state the motive for the journey as early as possible. Additional lines for the 'Garden of the Gods' are based on the translation of L. Oppenheim (*Orientalia* 17, 1948, 47–8). The same source gives the simile of the 'wool' for sleep. The 'Things of Stone' which Gilgamesh smashes before embarking with Urshanabi defy explanation at present. The sweet-water current along with the movements of Gilgamesh and Urshanabi when they leave Utnapishtim are difficult to follow; I have used a clue given by Speiser in *Ancient Near Eastern Texts* (p. 96, n. 232). The statement that Gilgamesh returned 'through the gate by which he had come' is taken from the words of the wife of Utnapishtim (Heidel XI, lines 207–8). Something is necessary here to mark the transition.

In the enumeration of names at the end of the Sumerian 'Death of Gilgamesh' I have left out two pairs which appear to belong to personages about whom nothing is known; for the others I have added an explanatory epithet, so that the names may convey a hint of what is implied in this catalogue. I have left them in their Sumerian forms. At three points I have borrowed a few lines from other epics. At the beginning of the account of the flood I have inserted the lines of explanation for the wrath of Enlil taken from the flood narrative in the Old Babylonian Atra-ḫasīs Epic (see below p. 57); they are the lines beginning 'In those days the world teemed, the people multiplied ...' Again at the end of Enkidu's dream of the underworld, the simile of the bailiff is taken from the Assyrian 'Vision of the Nether World', in which the whole passage has a fairly close parallel, while the lines describing the position of Dilmun come from the Sumerian 'Deluge'. A short résumé of the division of the material on the tablets will be found in the Appendix.

July 1959 (1972)   N. K. S.

Since the publication of this version of the Epic of Gilgamesh in 1960, decipherment of fresh tablets, and study of those already known, has added much to our understanding of the Epic itself, and of its historical and literary background. Gilgamesh was the subject of a meeting of the 'Rencontre Assyriologique Internationale', the proceedings of which have been published as *Gilgameš et sa légende*, Cahiers du Groupe François-Thureau-Dangin, 1, Paris 1960. Here are to be found a full bibliography, new textual material and discussions. Among the substantial additions of which, in spite of some contradictions, I have made use, is a new Sumerian account of the Humbaba (Huwawa) episode (J. van Dijk). The difficulties inseparable from this sort of interpretation can be seen in the fact that 'the felled cedars', and the tying and laying down of the branches, of one translation, have become, in another, 'aura coats', rosettes or 'sleeping camp-followers'. Another addition comes at a point where the text is particularly defective; the crisis of the meeting between Humbaba and Gilgamesh. To the Sumerian and Old Babylonian can now be added a Hittite tablet from Boghazköy, written down in the thirteenth century, and containing what is probably the Hurrian tradition concerning this episode, in which the hero may have been Humbaba, not Gilgamesh (H. Otten, 1958). The language is much like that known from other Hittite myths; and a single tablet covers the course of events from the endowing of Gilgamesh by the gods to the killing of Humbaba. This takes five tablets of Akkadian so there has been considerable compression; even so, some gaps are filled, as well as alternative matter provided at other points. It is, for example, perfectly natural that the Hittite weather-god should bestow the gift of courage in place of Akkadian Adad, to whom he holds an equivalent, though relatively superior, position. The trapper who snares Enkidu has an Akkadian name, Sangasu, meaning 'death-striker'; but more important is the possibility, hinted here, that Gilgamesh came to Uruk only after his earlier wanderings in the world, and so the resentment of his 'tyranny' becomes more understandable. The forest journey is given an actual physical setting. It starts from the banks of the Euphrates where the heroes make their sacrifice to the Sun God, and from there a six days' journey brings them to the Cedar Mountain. This is added confirmation for placing the mountain in a north westerly, rather than an easterly, direction, and agrees with the naming of Lebanon at the end of the fight with Humbaba in the Old Babylonian (Tell Iščali) fragment. But though in the Hittite tablet Humbaba threatens more alarmingly, the outcome is exactly the same and fits well between the Sumerian and Old

Babylonian fragments. Further details come from other sources and are published by A. Falkenstein (*Journal of Near Eastern Studies*, 19, April 1960, 2, 65–71) and J. van Dijk, (*Sumer*, 15, 1959, i, 8–10) but the differences are not more than may be expected in oral tradition. A tablet from Ur, perhaps of the eleventh century B.C., contains another version of, and additions to, part of Tablet VII of the Ninevite recension describing the conversation between Shamash and Enkidu on the latter's deathbed. It links up with the Sultantepe fragment and was published by C. J. Gadd in *Iraq*, 28, 1966, 105–121, with a commentary that includes interesting suggestions as to the name and character of 'Siduri', and consideration of the 'Stone Things' destroyed by Gilgamesh before crossing the Waters of Death.

Much of this new material has been incorporated into the text of the third edition of *Ancient Near Eastern Texts Relating to the Old Testament*, Princeton, New Jersey, 1969, or in the Supplement, pp. 503–7, translated by A. R. Grayson. A fragment of text from Tell Harmal gives the 'first' dream of Gilgamesh on the mountain and there are additions to the conversation between Gilgamesh and Ishtar, and the episode of the Bull of Heaven. Important new light is thrown on Enkidu's sickness and dreams by R. Stefanini (1969) Hittite material and by C. J. Gadd, *loc. cit.* (1966) with Middle Babylonian or Cassite period texts from Ur, perhaps of the early 11th century, which give an alternative to the Ninevite version and add considerably to the exchange between Enkidu and Shamash. The problem of the 'gate', whether it is still the 'gate of the forest', or whether it is not rather of forest wood but raised in Uruk, is discussed by I. M. Diakonoff (*Bibliotheca Orientalis*, XVIII, 1961, 61–67). I have taken the second alternative as most probable. The Stone Things are again discussed by C. J. Gadd, and by A. R. Millard (1964) publishing an Old Babylonian fragment which overlaps with Meissner, also D. Wiseman in *Gilgameš et sa légende* (1960). Minor additions to Tablet X are also taken from the new third edition of *Texts Relating to the Old Testament*, and I have followed suggestions in the article by L. Matouš (*Bibliotheca Orientalis*, XXI, 1964, 3–10) as well as from the various contributors to the article 'Gilgamesh' in the *Reallexikon der Assyriologie*, parts 3/4, pp. 357–74. A clue to the nature of the plant of eternal youth comes from R. Campbell Thompson's *Dictionary of Assyrian Botany* (London, 1949); and the amended first line of the epic is given in the *Assyrian Dictionary of the Oriental Institute of Chicago*, 7, 33b.

I have referred in this introduction to the discovery of new evidence for the existence of an historical Gilgamesh. The question is discussed, in *Gilgameš et sa légende*, by W. G. Lambert, S. N. Kramer and in a short note by E. O. Edzard; also M. Rowton, *Journal of Near Eastern Studies*, 19, 1960, 2, 156–62. The divergences, though important, are not very great, and whichever date is followed, Gilgamesh's lifetime will not be far from the date of the Royal Tombs of Ur with their refined wealth and barbaric ritual; thus the fragmentary Sumerian text of the 'Death of Gilgamesh' can be used as a semi-historical document to throw light on the funeral rites of the royal house of Ur in the third millennium, as in fact was done by Prof. Kramer in an article in *Iraq*, 22, 1960, 58. Prof. Mallowan has written on the subject of a flood or floods (*Iraq*, 26, 1964, 62–82) and it is also discussed in *Atra-ḫasīs, The Babylonian Story of the Flood* by W. G. Lambert and A. R. Millard (1969), with M. Civil on the Sumerian tradition of the flood.

The possible indebtedness of Greek mythology to the Orient has been treated in several recent books since T. B. L. Webster's *From Mycenae to Homer* (London, 1958): by P. Walcott, in *Hesiod and the Near East* (Cardiff, 1966), G. S. Kirk, *Myth, its Meaning and Functions in Ancient and Other Cultures* (Cambridge, 1970), and M. L. West, *Early Greek Philosophy and the Orient* (Oxford, 1971).

The question of who the Sumerians were is still unsolved and may remain so. If they were new arrivals they may not have been very numerous, and the extent of their influence on language and literature may never be really known.

May 1972 N. K. S.

The matter relating to Gilgamesh still grows. New texts come to light which add to our knowledge of the *Epic* and of the historical Gilgamesh, while work on the existing texts increases our understanding of difficult passages. Two outstanding works have appeared within recent years. Thorkild Jacobsen's *The Treasures of Darkness* (Newhaven and London, 1976), contains a fresh analysis of the whole *Epic* in the light of the author's general view of Mesopotamian religion; and J. H. Tigay in *The Evolution of the Gilgamesh Epic* (Philadelphia, 1982), by comparing versions and distinguishing different sources, both chronological and geographical, has shown how theological and political changes shaped the poem, and how the various strands came together in the final compilation. Interesting new light on the poem comes from W. G. Lambert in *The Theology of Death* (ed. B. Alster, XXVI Rencontre Assyriologique Internationale, 1980), and a new fragment from the fifth tablet is published by E. von Weiher in *Baghdader Mittheilungen* (1980, II, 90–105). R. A. Veenker has enlarged on the significance of the Magic Plant of Youth Restored as a separate myth in *Biblical Archaeologist* 1981, 44/45, 199–205), and so it continues. I am grateful to Mrs Stephanie Dalley for her help with the references.

September 1987 N. K. S.

ACKNOWLEDGEMENTS

To name all the authorities to whom I am indebted would
entail compiling a lengthy bibliography, but special mention
must be made of a few. I have received most valuable help from
Professor D. J. Wiseman, which has saved me from numerous
pitfalls; all the errors which remain are therefore my own. I owe
a large debt of gratitude to many friends who have criticized,
made suggestions, and given encouragement at different stages,
of the work; amongst these I thank particularly Ruth Harris,
Katherine Watson, and my sister; and above all I am grateful to
Dr E. V. Rieu for his patience, understanding, and encourage-
ment. I am only too aware of the many inperfections which
remain in this book, but without the help which has been given
so generously there would have been many more.

I gratefully acknowledge my debt to the following for per-
mission to use copyright material: Princeton University Press
(Publishers) for quotations from *Ancient New Eastern Texts
Relating to the Old Testament* edited by James B. Pritchard,
1950, 1955, 1969. Passages in my introduction are based
on excerpts from the following translations: *The Fields of
Paradise* and *The Good Fortune of the Dead* translated by John
A. Wilson; *Gudea: Ensi of Lagash* translated by A. Leo Oppen-
heim; *Enki and Ninhursag: A Paradise Myth* translated by
S. N. Kramer; *Hymn to Ishtar* and *Prayer of Lamentation to
Ishtar*, also *Prayer of Ashurbanipal to the Sun-God*, translated by
Ferris J. Stephens; *Atra-ḥasīs*, Lambert and Millard; and *A
Vision of the Nether World* translated by E. A. Speiser. I owe a
more general indebtedness to S. N. Kramer's translations of
Gilgamesh and the Land of the Living and *The Death of Gilgamesh*;
and to E. A. Speiser for the first eleven tablets of the Assyrian
recension of the Gilgamesh Epic, all published in *Ancient Near
Eastern Texts*. I owe as much also to A. Heidel and the University

ACKNOWLEDGEMENTS

Press of Chicago for permission to use and quote from *The Gilgamesh Epic and Old Testament Parallels*, copyright 1946 and 1949 by the University of Chicago. I thank Dr E. V. Rieu for permission to quote from his translation of *The Odyssey*, Penguin Classics, 1945, and the editors and publishers of the Loeb Classical Library, Harvard University, and William Heinemann, for quotations from H. G. Evelyn-White's *Hesiod*, 1950; also Professor Gwyn Jones for quotations from the translation of *The Mabinogion* by Gwyn and Thomas Jones, in the Everyman Library, J. M. Dent, 1949.

N. K. S.

THE EPIC OF GILGAMESH

*

GILGAMESH KING IN URUK

I WILL proclaim to the world the deeds of Gilgamesh. This was the man to whom all things were known; this was the king who knew the countries of the world. He was wise, he saw mysteries and knew secret things, he brought us a tale of the days before the flood. He went on a long journey, was weary, worn-out with labour, returning he rested, he engraved on a stone the whole story.

When the gods created Gilgamesh they gave him a perfect body. Shamash the glorious sun endowed him with beauty, Adad the god of the storm endowed him with courage, the great gods made his beauty perfect, surpassing all others, terrifying like a great wild bull. Two thirds they made him god and one third man.

In Uruk he built walls, a great rampart, and the temple of blessed Eanna for the god of the firmament Anu, and for Ishtar the goddess of love. Look at it still today: the outer wall where the cornice runs, it shines with the brilliance of copper; and the inner wall, it has no equal. Touch the threshold, it is ancient. Approach Eanna the dwelling of Ishtar, our lady of love and war, the like of which no latter-day king, no man alive can equal. Climb upon the wall of Uruk; walk along it, I say; regard the foundation terrace and examine the masonry: is it not burnt brick and good? The seven sages laid the foundations.

I

THE COMING OF ENKIDU

GILGAMESH went abroad in the world, but he met with none who could withstand his arms till he came to Uruk. But the men of Uruk muttered in their houses, 'Gilgamesh sounds the tocsin for his amusement, his arrogance has no bounds by day or night. No son is left with his father, for Gilgamesh takes them all, even the children; yet the king should be a shepherd to his people. His lust leaves no virgin to her lover, neither the warrior's daughter nor the wife of the noble; yet this is the shepherd of the city, wise, comely, and resolute.'

The gods heard their lament, the gods of heaven cried to the Lord of Uruk, to Anu the god of Uruk: 'A goddess made him, strong as a savage bull, none can withstand his arms. No son is left with his father, for Gilgamesh takes them all; and is this the king, the shepherd of his people? His lust leaves no virgin to her lover, neither the warrior's daughter nor the wife of the noble.' When Anu had heard their lamentation the gods cried to Aruru, the goddess of creation, 'You made him, O Aruru, now create his equal; let it be as like him as his own reflection, his second self, stormy heart for stormy heart. Let them contend together and leave Uruk in quiet.'

So the goddess conceived an image in her mind, and it was of the stuff of Anu of the firmament. She dipped her hands in water and pinched off clay, she let it fall in the wilderness, and noble Enkidu was created. There was virtue in him of the god of war, of Ninurta himself. His body was rough, he had long hair like a woman's; it waved like the hair of Nisaba, the goddess of corn. His body was covered with matted hair like Samuqan's, the god of cattle. He was innocent of mankind; he knew nothing of the cultivated land.

Enkidu ate grass in the hills with the gazelle and lurked with wild beasts at the water-holes; he had joy of the water with the herds of wild game. But there was a trapper who met him one day face to face at the drinking-hole, for the wild game had entered his territory. On three days he met him face to face, and the trapper was frozen with fear. He went back to his house with the game that he had caught, and he was dumb, benumbed with terror. His face was altered like that of one who has made a long journey. With awe in his heart he spoke to his father: 'Father, there is a man, unlike any other, who comes down from the hills. He is the strongest in the world, he is like an immortal from heaven. He ranges over the hills with wild beasts and eats grass; he ranges through your land and comes down to the wells. I am afraid and dare not go near him. He fills in the pits which I dig and tears up my traps set for the game; he helps the beasts to escape and now they slip through my fingers.'

His father opened his mouth and said to the trapper, 'My son, in Uruk lives Gilgamesh; no one has ever prevailed against him, he is strong as a star from heaven. Go to Uruk, find Gilgamesh, extol the strength of this wild man. Ask him to give you a harlot, a wanton from the temple of love; return with her, and let her woman's power overpower this man. When next he comes down to drink at the wells she will be there, stripped naked; and when he sees her beckoning he will embrace her, and then the wild beasts will reject him.'

So the trapper set out on his journey to Uruk and addressed himself to Gilgamesh saying, 'A man unlike any other is roaming now in the pastures; he is as strong as a star from heaven and I am afraid to approach him. He helps the wild game to escape; he fills in my pits and pulls up my traps.' Gilgamesh said, 'Trapper, go back, take with you a harlot, a child of pleasure. At the drinking-hole she will strip, and when he sees her beckoning he will embrace her and the game of the wilderness will surely reject him.'

Now the trapper returned, taking the harlot with him. After a three days' journey they came to the drinking-hole, and there they sat down; the harlot and the trapper sat facing one another and waited for the game to come. For the first day and for the second day the two sat waiting, but on the third day the herds came; they came down to drink and Enkidu was with them. The small wild creatures of the plains were glad of the water, and Enkidu with them, who ate grass with the gazelle and was born in the hills; and she saw him, the savage man, come from far-off in the hills. The trapper spoke to her: 'There he is. Now, woman, make your breasts bare, have no shame, do not delay but welcome his love. Let him see you naked, let him possess your body. When he comes near uncover yourself and lie with him; teach him, the savage man, your woman's art, for when he murmurs love to you the wild beasts that shared his life in the hills will reject him.'

She was not ashamed to take him, she made herself naked and welcomed his eagerness; as he lay on her murmuring love she taught him the woman's art. For six days and seven nights they lay together, for Enkidu had forgotten his home in the hills; but when he was satisfied he went back to the wild beasts. Then, when the gazelle saw him, they bolted away; when the wild creatures saw him they fled. Enkidu would have followed, but his body was bound as though with a cord, his knees gave way when he started to run, his swiftness was gone. And now the wild creatures had all fled away; Enkidu was grown weak, for wisdom was in him, and the thoughts of a man were in his heart. So he returned and sat down at the woman's feet, and listened intently to what she said. 'You are wise, Enkidu, and now you have become like a god. Why do you want to run wild with the beasts in the hills? Come with me. I will take you to strong-walled Uruk, to the blessed temple of Ishtar and of Anu, of love and of heaven: there Gilgamesh lives, who is very strong, and like a wild bull he lords it over men.'

When she had spoken Enkidu was pleased; he longed for a comrade, for one who would understand his heart. 'Come, woman, and take me to that holy temple, to the house of Anu and of Ishtar, and to the place where Gilgamesh lords it over the people. I will challenge him boldly, I will cry out aloud in Uruk, "I am the strongest here, I have come to change the old order, I am he who was born in the hills, I am he who is strongest of all."'

She said, 'Let us go, and let him see your face. I know very well where Gilgamesh is in great Uruk. O Enkidu, there all the people are dressed in their gorgeous robes, every day is holiday, the young men and the girls are wonderful to see. How sweet they smell! All the great ones are roused from their beds. O Enkidu, you who love life, I will show you Gilgamesh, a man of many moods;

you shall look at him well in his radiant manhood. His body is perfect in strength and maturity; he never rests by night or day. He is stronger than you, so leave your boasting. Shamash the glorious sun has given favours to Gilgamesh, and Anu of the heavens, and Enlil, and Ea the wise has given him deep understanding. I tell you, even before you have left the wilderness, Gilgamesh will know in his dreams that you are coming.'

Now Gilgamesh got up to tell his dream to his mother, Ninsun, one of the wise gods. 'Mother, last night I had a dream. I was full of joy, the young heroes were round me and I walked through the night under the stars of the firmament, and one, a meteor of the stuff of Anu, fell down from heaven. I tried to lift it but it proved too heavy. All the people of Uruk came round to see it, the common people jostled and the nobles thronged to kiss its feet; and to me its attraction was like the love of woman. They helped me, I braced my forehead and I raised it with thongs and brought it to you, and you yourself pronounced it my brother.'

Then Ninsun, who is well-beloved and wise, said to Gilgamesh, 'This star of heaven which descended like a meteor from the sky; which you tried to lift, but found too heavy, when you tried to move it it would not budge, and so you brought it to my feet; I made it for you, a goad and spur, and you were drawn as though to a woman. This is the strong comrade, the one who brings help to his friend in his need. He is the strongest of wild creatures, the stuff of Anu; born in the grass-lands and the wild hills reared him; when you see him you will be glad; you will love him as a woman and he will never forsake you. This is the meaning of the dream.'

Gilgamesh said, 'Mother, I dreamed a second dream. In the streets of strong-walled Uruk there lay an axe; the shape of it was strange and the people thronged round. I saw it and was glad. I bent down, deeply drawn towards it; I loved it like a woman and wore it at my side.' Ninsun answered, 'That axe, which you saw, which drew you so powerfully like love of a woman, that is the comrade whom I give you, and he will come in his strength like one of the host of heaven. He is the brave companion who rescues his friend in necessity.' Gilgamesh said to his mother, 'A friend, a counsellor has come to me from Enlil, and now I shall befriend and counsel him.' So Gilgamesh told his dreams; and the harlot retold them to Enkidu.

And now she said to Enkidu, 'When I look at you you have become like a god. Why do you yearn to run wild again with the beasts in the hills? Get up from the ground, the bed of a shepherd.' He listened to her words with care. It was good advice that she gave. She divided her clothing in two and with the one half she clothed him and with the other herself; and holding his hand she led him like a child to the sheepfolds, into the shepherds' tents. There all the shepherds crowded round to see him, they put down bread in front of him, but Enkidu could only suck the milk of wild animals. He fumbled and gaped, at a loss what to do or how he should eat the bread and drink the strong wine. Then the woman said, 'Enkidu, eat bread, it is the staff of life; drink the wine, it is the custom of the land.' So he ate till he was full and drank strong wine, seven goblets. He became merry, his heart exulted and his face shone. He rubbed down the matted hair of his body and anointed himself with oil. Enkidu had become a man; but when he had put on man's clothing he appeared like a bridegroom.

He took arms to hunt the lion so that the shepherds could rest at night. He caught wolves and lions and the herdsmen lay down in peace; for Enkidu was their watchman, that strong man who had no rival.

He was merry living with the shepherds, till one day lifting his eyes he saw a man approaching. He said to the harlot, 'Woman, fetch that man here. Why has he come? I wish to know his name.' She went and called the man saying, 'Sir, where are you going on this weary journey?' The man answered, saying to Enkidu, 'Gilgamesh has gone into the marriage-house and shut out the people. He does strange things in Uruk, the city of great streets. At the roll of the drum work begins for the men, and work for the women. Gilgamesh the king is about to celebrate marriage with the Queen of Love, and he still demands to be first with the bride, the king to be first and the husband to follow, for that was ordained by the gods from his birth, from the time the umbilical cord was cut. But now the drums roll for the choice of the bride and the city groans.' At these words Enkidu turned white in the face. 'I will go to the place where Gilgamesh lords it over the people, I will challenge him boldly, and I will cry aloud in Uruk, "I have come to change the old order, for I am the strongest here."'

Now Enkidu strode in front and the woman followed behind. He entered Uruk, that great market, and all the folk thronged round him where he stood in the street in strong-walled Uruk. The people jostled; speaking of him they said, 'He is the spit of Gilgamesh.' 'He is shorter.' 'He is bigger of bone.' 'This is the one who was reared on the milk of wild beasts. His is the greatest strength.' The men rejoiced: 'Now Gilgamesh has met his match. This great one, this hero whose beauty is like a god, he is a match even for Gilgamesh.'

In Uruk the bridal bed was made, fit for the goddess of love. The bride waited for the bridegroom, but in the night Gilgamesh got up and came to the house. Then Enkidu stepped out, he stood in the street and blocked the way. Mighty Gilgamesh came on and Enkidu met him at the gate. He put out his foot and prevented Gilgamesh from entering the house, so they grappled, holding each other like bulls. They broke the doorposts and the walls shook, they snorted like bulls locked together. They shattered the doorposts and the walls shook. Gilgamesh bent his knee with his foot planted on the ground and with a turn Enkidu was thrown. Then immediately his fury died. When Enkidu was thrown he said to Gilgamesh, 'There is not another like you in the world. Ninsun, who is as strong as a wild ox in the byre, she was the mother who bore you, and now you are raised above all men, and Enlil has given you the kingship, for your strength surpasses the strength of men.' So Enkidu and Gilgamesh embraced and their friendship was sealed.

2

THE FOREST JOURNEY

ENLIL of the mountain, the father of the gods, had decreed the destiny of Gilgamesh. So Gilgamesh dreamed and Enkidu said, 'The meaning of the dream is this. The father of the gods has given you kingship, such is your destiny, everlasting life is not your destiny. Because of this do not be sad at heart, do not be grieved or oppressed. He has given you power to bind and to loose, to be the darkness and the light of mankind. He has given you unexampled supremacy over the people, victory in battle from which no fugitive returns, in forays and assaults from which there is no going back. But do not abuse this power, deal justly with your servants in the palace, deal justly before Shamash.'

The eyes of Enkidu were full of tears and his heart was sick. He sighed bitterly and Gilgamesh met his eye and said, 'My friend, why do you sigh so bitterly?' But Enkidu opened his mouth and said, 'I am weak, my arms have lost their strength, the cry of sorrow sticks in my throat, I am oppressed by idleness.' It was then that the lord Gilgamesh turned his thoughts to the Country of the Living; on the Land of Cedars the lord Gilgamesh reflected. He said to his servant Enkidu, 'I have not established my name stamped on bricks as my destiny decreed; therefore I will go to the country where the cedar is felled. I will set up my name in the place where the names of famous men are written, and where no man's name is written yet I will

raise a monument to the gods. Because of the evil that is
in the land, we will go to the forest and destroy the evil;
for in the forest lives Humbaba whose name is "Huge-
ness", a ferocious giant.' But Enkidu sighed bitterly and
said, 'When I went with the wild beasts ranging through
the wilderness I discovered the forest; its length is ten
thousand leagues in every direction. Enlil has appointed
Humbaba to guard it and armed him in sevenfold terrors,
terrible to all flesh is Humbaba. When he roars it is like the
torrent of the storm, his breath is like fire, and his jaws are
death itself. He guards the cedars so well that when the
wild heifer stirs in the forest, though she is sixty leagues
distant, he hears her. What man would willingly walk into
that country and explore its depths? I tell you, weakness
overpowers whoever goes near it: it is not an equal
struggle when one fights with Humbaba; he is a great
warrior, a battering-ram. Gilgamesh, the watchman of the
forest never sleeps.'

Gilgamesh replied: 'Where is the man who can clamber
to heaven? Only the gods live for ever with glorious
Shamash, but as for us men, our days are numbered, our
occupations are a breath of wind. How is this, already you
are afraid! I will go first although I am your lord, and you
may safely call out, "Forward, there is nothing to fear!"
Then if I fall I leave behind me a name that endures; men
will say of me, "Gilgamesh has fallen in fight with
ferocious Humbaba." Long after the child has been born
in my house, they will say it, and remember.' Enkidu
spoke again to Gilgamesh, 'O my lord, if you will enter
that country, go first to the hero Shamash, tell the Sun
God, for the land is his. The country where the cedar is cut
belongs to Shamash.'

Gilgamesh took up a kid, white without spot, and a brown one with it; he held them against his breast, and he carried them into the presence of the sun. He took in his hand his silver sceptre and he said to glorious Shamash, 'I am going to that country, O Shamash, I am going; my hands supplicate, so let it be well with my soul and bring me back to the quay of Uruk. Grant, I beseech, your protection, and let the omen be good.' Glorious Shamash answered, 'Gilgamesh, you are strong, but what is the Country of the Living to you?'

'O Shamash, hear me, hear me, Shamash, let my voice be heard. Here in the city man dies oppressed at heart, man perishes with despair in his heart. I have looked over the wall and I see the bodies floating on the river, and that will be my lot also. Indeed I know it is so, for whoever is tallest among men cannot reach the heavens, and the greatest cannot encompass the earth. Therefore I would enter that country: because I have not established my name stamped on brick as my destiny decreed, I will go to the country where the cedar is cut. I will set up my name where the names of famous men are written; and where no man's name is written I will raise a monument to the gods.' The tears ran down his face and he said, 'Alas, it is a long journey that I must take to the Land of Humbaba. If this enterprise is not to be accomplished, why did you move me, Shamash, with the restless desire to perform it? How can I succeed if you will not succour me? If I die in that country I will die without rancour, but if I return I will make a glorious offering of gifts and of praise to Shamash.'

So Shamash accepted the sacrifice of his tears; like the compassionate man he showed him mercy. He appointed strong allies for Gilgamesh, sons of one mother, and stationed them in the mountain caves. The great winds he appointed: the north wind, the whirlwind, the storm and the icy wind, the tempest and the scorching wind. Like vipers, like dragons, like a scorching fire, like a serpent that freezes the heart, a destroying flood and the lightning's fork, such were they and Gilgamesh rejoiced.

He went to the forge and said, 'I will give orders to the armourers; they shall cast us our weapons while we watch them.' So they gave orders to the armourers and the craftsmen sat down in conference. They went into the groves of the plain and cut willow and box-wood; they cast for them axes of nine score pounds, and great swords they cast with blades of six score pounds each one, with pommels and hilts of thirty pounds. They cast for Gilgamesh the axe 'Might of Heroes' and the bow of Anshan; and Gilgamesh was armed and Enkidu; and the weight of the arms they carried was thirty score pounds.

The people collected and the counsellors in the streets and in the market-place of Uruk; they came through the gate of seven bolts and Gilgamesh spoke to them in the market-place: 'I, Gilgamesh, go to see that creature of whom such things are spoken, the rumour of whose name fills the world. I will conquer him in his cedar wood and show the strength of the sons of Uruk, all the world shall know of it. I am committed to this enterprise: to climb the mountain, to cut down the cedar, and leave behind me an enduring name.' The counsellors of Uruk, the great market, answered him, 'Gilgamesh, you are young, your courage carries you too far, you cannot know what this enterprise means which you plan. We have heard that Humbaba is not like men who die, his weapons are such that none can stand against them; the forest stretches for ten thousand leagues in every direction; who would willingly go down to explore its depths? As for Humbaba, when he roars it is like the torrent of the storm, his breath is like fire and his jaws are death itself. Why do you crave to do this thing, Gilgamesh? It is no equal struggle when one fights with Humbaba, that battering-ram.'

When he heard these words of the counsellors Gilgamesh looked at his friend and laughed, 'How shall I answer them; shall I say I am afraid of Humbaba, I will sit at home all the rest of my days?' Then Gilgamesh opened his mouth again and said to Enkidu, 'My friend, let us go to the Great Palace, to Egalmah, and stand before Ninsun the queen. Ninsun is wise with deep knowledge, she will give us counsel for the road we must go.' They took each other by the hand as they went to Egalmah, and they went to Ninsun the great queen. Gilgamesh approached, he entered the palace and spoke to Ninsun. 'Ninsun, will you listen to me; I have a long journey to go, to the Land of Humbaba, I must travel an unknown road and fight a strange battle. From the day I go until I return, till I reach the cedar forest and destroy the evil which Shamash abhors, pray for me to Shamash.'

Ninsun went into her room, she put on a dress becoming to her body, she put on jewels to make her breast beautiful, she placed a tiara on her head and her skirts swept the ground. Then she went up to the altar of the Sun, standing upon the roof of the palace; she burnt incense and lifted her arms to Shamash as the smoke ascended: 'O Shamash, why did you give this restless heart to Gilgamesh, my son; why did you give it? You have moved him and now he sets out on a long journey to the Land of Humbaba, to travel an unknown road and fight a strange battle. Therefore from the day that he goes till the day he returns, until he reaches the cedar forest, until he kills Humbaba and destroys the evil thing which you, Shamash, abhor, do not forget him; but let the dawn, Aya, your dear bride, remind you always, and when day is done give him to the watch-man of the night to keep him from harm.' Then Ninsun the mother of Gilgamesh extinguished the incense, and she called to Enkidu with this exhortation: 'Strong Enkidu, you are not the child of my body, but I will receive you as my adopted son; you are my other child like the foundlings they bring to the temple. Serve Gilgamesh as a foundling serves the temple and the priestess who reared him. In the presence of my women, my votaries and hierophants, I declare it.' Then she placed the amulet for a pledge round his neck, and she said to him, 'I entrust my son to you; bring him back to me safely.'

And now they brought to them the weapons, they put in their hands the great swords in their golden scabbards, and the bow and the quiver. Gilgamesh took the axe, he slung the quiver from his shoulder, and the bow of Anshan, and buckled the sword to his belt; and so they were armed and ready for the journey. Now all the people came and pressed on them and said, 'When will you return to the city?' The counsellors blessed Gilgamesh and warned him, 'Do not trust too much in your own strength, be watchful, restrain your blows at first. The one who goes in front protects his companion; the good guide who knows the way guards his friend. Let Enkidu lead the way, he knows the road to the forest, he has seen Humbaba and is experienced in battles; let him press first into the passes, let him be watchful and look to himself.

Let Enkidu protect his friend, and guard his companion, and bring him safe through the pitfalls of the road. We, the counsellors of Uruk entrust our king to you, O Enkidu; bring him back safely to us.' Again to Gilgamesh they said, 'May Shamash give you your heart's desire, may he let you see with your eyes the thing accomplished which your lips have spoken; may he open a path for you where it is blocked, and a road for your feet to tread. May he open the mountains for your crossing, and may the night-time bring you the blessings of night, and Lugulbanda, your guardian god, stand beside you for victory. May you have victory in the battle as though you fought with a child. Wash your feet in the river of Humbaba to which you are journeying; in the evening dig a well, and let there always be pure water in your water-skin. Offer cold water to Shamash and do not forget Lugulbanda.'

Then Enkidu opened his mouth and said, 'Forward, there is nothing to fear. Follow me, for I know the place where Humbaba lives and the paths where he walks. Let the counsellors go back. Here is no cause for fear.' When the counsellors heard this they sped the hero on his way. 'Go, Gilgamesh, may your guardian god protect you on the road and bring you safely back to the quay of Uruk.'

After twenty leagues they broke their fast; after another thirty leagues they stopped for the night. Fifty leagues they walked in one day; in three days they had walked as much as a journey of a month and two weeks. They crossed seven mountains before they came to the gate of the forest. Then Enkidu called out to Gilgamesh, 'Do not go down into the forest; when I opened the gate my hand lost its strength.' Gilgamesh answered him, 'Dear friend, do not speak like a coward. Have we got the better of so many dangers and travelled so far, to turn back at last? You, who are tried in wars and battles, hold close to me now and you will feel no fear of death; keep beside me and your weakness will pass, the trembling will leave your hand. Would my friend rather stay behind? No, we will go down together into the heart of the forest. Let your courage be roused by the battle to come; forget death and follow me, a man resolute in action, but one who is not foolhardy. When two go together each will protect himself and shield his companion, and if they fall they leave an enduring name.'

Together they went down into the forest and they came to the green mountain. There they stood still, they were struck dumb; they stood still and gazed at the forest. They saw the height of the cedar, they saw the way into the forest and the track where Humbaba was used to walk. The way was broad and the going was good. They gazed at the mountain of cedars, the dwelling-place of the gods and the throne of Ishtar. The hugeness of the cedar rose in front of the mountain, its shade was beautiful, full of comfort; mountain and glade were green with brushwood.

There Gilgamesh dug a well before the setting sun. He went up the mountain and poured out fine meal on the ground and said, 'O mountain, dwelling of the gods, bring me a favourable dream.' Then they took each other by the hand and lay down to sleep; and sleep that flows from the night lapped over them. Gilgamesh dreamed, and at midnight sleep left him, and he told his dream to his friend. 'Enkidu, what was it that woke me if you did not? My friend, I have dreamed a dream. Get up, look at the mountain precipice. The sleep that the gods sent me is broken. Ah, my friend, what a dream I have had! Terror and confusion; I seized hold of a wild bull in the wilderness. It bellowed and beat up the dust till the whole sky was dark, my arm was seized and my tongue bitten. I fell back on my knee; then someone refreshed me with water from his water-skin.'

Enkidu said, 'Dear friend, the god to whom we are travelling is no wild bull, though his form is mysterious. That wild bull which you saw is Shamash the Protector; in our moment of peril he will take our hands. The one who gave water from his water-skin, that is your own god who cares for your good name, your Lugulbanda. United with him, together we will accomplish a work the fame of which will never die.'

Gilgamesh said, 'I dreamed again. We stood in a deep gorge of the mountain, and beside it we two were like the smallest of swamp flies; and suddenly the mountain fell, it struck me and caught my feet from under me. Then came an intolerable light blazing out, and in it was one whose grace and whose beauty were greater than the beauty of this world. He pulled me out from under the mountain, he gave me water to drink and my heart was comforted, and he set my feet on the ground.'

Then Enkidu the child of the plains said, 'Let us go down from the mountain and talk this thing over together.' He said to Gilgamesh the young god, 'Your dream is good, your dream is excellent, the mountain which you saw is Humbaba. Now, surely, we will seize and kill him, and throw his body down as the mountain fell on the plain.'

The next day after twenty leagues they broke their fast, and after another thirty they stopped for the night. They dug a well before the sun had set and Gilgamesh ascended the mountain. He poured out fine meal on the ground and said, 'O mountain, dwelling of the gods, send a dream for Enkidu, make him a favourable dream.' The mountain fashioned a dream for Enkidu; it came, an ominous dream; a cold shower passed over him, it caused him to cower like the mountain barley under a storm of rain. But Gilgamesh sat with his chin on his knees till the sleep which flows over all mankind lapped over him. Then, at midnight, sleep left him; he got up and said to his friend, 'Did you call me, or why did I wake? Did you touch me, or why am I terrified? Did not some god pass by, for my limbs are numb with fear? My friend, I saw a third dream and this dream was altogether frightful. The heavens roared and the earth roared again, daylight failed and darkness fell, lightnings flashed, fire blazed out, the clouds lowered, they rained down death. Then the brightness departed, the fire went out, and all was turned to ashes fallen about us. Let us go down from the mountain and talk this over, and consider what we should do.'

When they had come down from the mountain Gilgamesh seized the axe in his hand: he felled the cedar. When Humbaba heard the noise far off he was enraged; he cried out, 'Who is this that has violated my woods and cut down my cedar?' But glorious Shamash called to them out of heaven, 'Go forward, do not be afraid.' But now Gilgamesh was overcome by weakness, for sleep had seized him suddenly, a profound sleep held him; he lay on the ground, stretched out speechless, as though in a dream. When Enkidu touched him he did not rise, when he spoke to him he did not reply. 'O Gilgamesh, Lord of the plain of Kullab, the world grows dark, the shadows have spread over it, now is the glimmer of dusk. Shamash has departed, his bright head is quenched in the bosom of his mother

79

Ningal. O Gilgamesh, how long will you lie like this, asleep? Never let the mother who gave you birth be forced in mourning into the city square.'

At length Gilgamesh heard him; he put on his breastplate, 'The Voice of Heroes', of thirty shekels' weight; he put it on as though it had been a light garment that he carried, and it covered him altogether. He straddled the earth like a bull that snuffs the ground and his teeth were clenched. 'By the life of my mother Ninsun who gave me birth, and by the life of my father, divine Lugulbanda, let me live to be the wonder of my mother, as when she nursed me on her lap.' A second time he said to him, 'By the life of Ninsun my mother who gave me birth, and by the life of my father, divine Lugulbanda, until we have fought this man, if man he is, this god, if god he is, the way that I took to the Country of the Living will not turn back to the city.'

Then Enkidu, the faithful companion, pleaded, answering him, 'O my lord, you do not know this monster and that is the reason you are not afraid. I who know him, I am terrified. His teeth are dragon's fangs, his countenance is like a lion, his charge is the rushing of the flood, with his look he crushes alike the trees of the forest and reeds in the swamp. O my Lord, you may go on if you choose into this land, but I will go back to the city. I will tell the lady your mother all your glorious deeds till she shouts for joy: and then I will tell the death that followed till she weeps for bitterness.' But Gilgamesh said, 'Immolation and sacrifice are not yet for me, the boat of the dead shall not go down, nor the three-ply cloth be cut for my shrouding. Not yet will my people be desolate, nor the pyre be lit in my house and my dwelling burnt on the fire.

Today, give me your aid and you shall have mine: what then can go amiss with us two? All living creatures born of the flesh shall sit at last in the boat of the West, and when it sinks, when the boat of Magilum sinks, they are gone; but we shall go forward and fix our eyes on this monster. If your heart is fearful throw away fear; if there is terror in it throw away terror. Take your axe in your hand and attack. He who leaves the fight unfinished is not at peace.'

Humbaba came out from his strong house of cedar. Then Enkidu called out, 'O Gilgamesh, remember now your boasts in Uruk. Forward, attack, son of Uruk, there is nothing to fear.' When he heard these words his courage rallied; he answered, 'Make haste, close in, if the watchman is there do not let him escape to the woods where he will vanish. He has put on the first of his seven splendours but not yet the other six, let us trap him before he is armed.' Like a raging wild bull he snuffed the ground; the watchman of the woods turned full of threatenings, he cried out. Humbaba came from his strong house of cedar. He nodded his head and shook it, menacing Gilgamesh; and on him he fastened his eye, the eye of death. Then Gilgamesh called to Shamash and his tears were flowing, 'O glorious Shamash, I have followed the road you commanded but now if you send no succour how shall I escape?' Glorious Shamash heard his prayer and he summoned the great wind, the north wind, the whirlwind, the storm and the icy wind, the tempest and the scorching wind; they came like dragons, like a scorching fire, like a serpent that freezes the heart, a destroying flood and the lightning's fork. The eight winds rose up against Humbaba, they beat against his eyes; he was gripped, unable to go forward or back. Gilgamesh shouted, 'By the life of Ninsun my mother

and divine Lugulbanda my father, in the Country of the
Living, in this Land I have discovered your dwelling; my
weak arms and my small weapons I have brought to this
Land against you, and now I will enter your house'.

So he felled the first cedar and they cut the branches
and laid them at the foot of the mountain. At the first
stroke Humbaba blazed out, but still they advanced. They
felled seven cedars and cut and bound the branches and
laid them at the foot of the mountain, and seven times
Humbaba loosed his glory on them. As the seventh blaze
died out they reached his lair. He slapped his thigh in
scorn. He approached like a noble wild bull roped on the
mountain, a warrior whose elbows are bound together.
The tears started to his eyes and he was pale, 'Gilgamesh,
let me speak. I have never known a mother, no, nor a
father who reared me. I was born of the mountain, he
reared me, and Enlil made me the keeper of this forest.
Let me go free, Gilgamesh, and I will be your servant,
you shall be my lord; all the trees of the forest that I tended
on the mountain shall be yours. I will cut them down and
build you a palace.' He took him by the hand and led him
to his house, so that the heart of Gilgamesh was moved
with compassion. He swore by the heavenly life, by the
earthly life, by the underworld itself: 'O Enkidu, should
not the snared bird return to its nest and the captive man
return to his mother's arms?' Enkidu answered, 'The
strongest of men will fall to fate if he has no judgement.
Namtar, the evil fate that knows no distinction between
men, will devour him. If the snared bird returns to its
nest, if the captive man returns to his mother's arms, then
you my friend will never return to the city where the
mother is waiting who gave you birth. He will bar the

mountain road against you, and make the pathways impassable.'

Humbaba said, 'Enkidu, what you have spoken is evil: you, a hireling, dependent for your bread! In envy and for fear of a rival you have spoken evil words.' Enkidu said, 'Do not listen, Gilgamesh: this Humbaba must die. Kill Humbaba first and his servants after.' But Gilgamesh said, 'If we touch him the blaze and the glory of light will be put out in confusion, the glory and glamour will vanish, its rays will be quenched.' Enkidu said to Gilgamesh, 'Not so, my friend. First entrap the bird, and where shall the chicks run then? Afterwards we can search out the glory and the glamour, when the chicks run distracted through the grass.'

Gilgamesh listened to the word of his companion, he took the axe in his hand, he drew the sword from his belt, and he struck Humbaba with a thrust of the sword to the neck, and Enkidu his comrade struck the second blow. At the third blow Humbaba fell. Then there followed confusion for this was the guardian of the forest whom they had felled to the ground. For as far as two leagues the cedars shivered when Enkidu felled the watcher of the forest, he at whose voice Hermon and Lebanon used to tremble. Now the mountains were moved and all the hills, for the guardian of the forest was killed. They attacked the cedars, the seven splendours of Humbaba were extinguished. So they pressed on into the forest bearing the sword of eight talents. They uncovered the sacred dwellings of the Anunnaki and while Gilgamesh felled the first of the trees of the forest Enkidu cleared their roots as far as the banks of Euphrates. They set Humbaba before the gods, before Enlil; they kissed the ground and dropped the shroud and set the head before him. When he saw the head of Humbaba, Enlil raged at them. 'Why did you do this thing? From henceforth may the fire be on your faces, may it eat the bread that you eat, may it drink where you drink.' Then Enlil took again the blaze and the seven splendours that had been Humbaba's: he gave the first to the river, and he gave to the lion, to the stone of execration, to the mountain and to the dreaded daughter of the Queen of Hell.

O Gilgamesh, king and conqueror of the dreadful blaze; wild bull who plunders the mountain, who crosses the sea, glory to him, and from the brave the greater glory is Enki's!

3

ISHTAR AND GILGAMESH, AND
THE DEATH OF ENKIDU

GILGAMESH washed out his long locks and cleaned his weapons; he flung back his hair from his shoulders; he threw off his stained clothes and changed them for new. He put on his royal robes and made them fast. When Gilgamesh had put on the crown, glorious Ishtar lifted her eyes, seeing the beauty of Gilgamesh. She said, 'Come to me Gilgamesh, and be my bridegroom; grant me seed of your body, let me be your bride and you shall be my husband. I will harness for you a chariot of lapis lazuli and of gold, with wheels of gold and horns of copper; and you shall have mighty demons of the storm for draft-mules. When you enter our house in the fragrance of cedar-wood, threshold and throne will kiss your feet. Kings, rulers, and princes will bow down before you; they shall bring you tribute from the mountains and the plain. Your ewes shall drop twins and your goats triplets; your pack-ass shall outrun mules; your oxen shall have no rivals, and your chariot horses shall be famous far-off for their swiftness.'

Gilgamesh opened his mouth and answered glorious Ishtar, 'If I take you in marriage, what gifts can I give in return? What ointments and clothing for your body? I would gladly give you bread and all sorts of food fit for a

god. I would give you wine to drink fit for a queen. I
would pour out barley to stuff your granary; but as for
making you my wife – that I will not. How would it go
with me? Your lovers have found you like a brazier which
smoulders in the cold, a backdoor which keeps out neither
squall of wind nor storm, a castle which crushes the
garrison, pitch that blackens the bearer, a water-skin that
chafes the carrier, a stone which falls from the parapet, a
battering-ram turned back from the enemy, a sandal that
trips the wearer. Which of your lovers did you ever love
for ever? What shepherd of yours has pleased you for all
time? Listen to me while I tell the tale of your lovers.
There was Tammuz, the lover of your youth, for him
you decreed wailing, year after year. You loved the many-
coloured roller, but still you struck and broke his wing;
now in the grove he sits and cries, "kappi, kappi, my
wing, my wing." You have loved the lion tremendous in
strength: seven pits you dug for him, and seven. You have
loved the stallion magnificent in battle, and for him you
decreed whip and spur and a thong, to gallop seven leagues
by force and to muddy the water before he drinks; and
for his mother Silili lamentations. You have loved the
shepherd of the flock; he made meal-cake for you day
after day, he killed kids for your sake. You struck and
turned him into a wolf; now his own herd-boys chase
him away, his own hounds worry his flanks. And did you
not love Ishullanu, the gardener of your father's palm-
grove? He brought you baskets filled with dates without
end; every day he loaded your table. Then you turned
your eyes on him and said, "Dearest Ishullanu, come here
to me, let us enjoy your manhood, come forward and
take me, I am yours." Ishullanu answered, "What are you

asking from me? My mother has baked and I have eaten; why should I come to such as you for food that is tainted and rotten? For when was a screen of rushes sufficient protection from frosts?" But when you had heard his answer you struck him. He was changed to a blind mole deep in the earth, one whose desire is always beyond his reach. And if you and I should be lovers, should not I be served in the same fashion as all these others whom you loved once?'

When Ishtar heard this she fell into a bitter rage, she went up to high heaven. Her tears poured down in front of her father Anu, and Antum her mother. She said, 'My father, Gilgamesh has heaped insults on me, he has told over all my abominable behaviour, my foul and hideous acts.' Anu opened his mouth and said, 'Are you a father of gods? Did not you quarrel with Gilgamesh the king, so now he has related your abominable behaviour, your foul and hideous acts.'

Ishtar opened her mouth and said again, 'My father, give me the Bull of Heaven to destroy Gilgamesh. Fill Gilgamesh, I say, with arrogance to his destruction; but if you refuse to give me the Bull of Heaven I will break in the doors of hell and smash the bolts; there will be confusion of people, those above with those from the lower depths. I shall bring up the dead to eat food like the living; and the hosts of dead will outnumber the living.' Anu said to great Ishtar, 'If I do what you desire there will be seven years of drought throughout Uruk when corn will be seedless husks. Have you saved grain enough for the people and grass for the cattle?' Ishtar replied. 'I have saved grain for the people, grass for the cattle; for seven years of seedless husks there is grain and there is grass enough.'

When Anu heard what Ishtar had said he gave her the Bull of Heaven to lead by the halter down to Uruk. When they reached the gates of Uruk the Bull went to the river; with his first snort cracks opened in the earth and a hundred young men fell down to death. With his second snort cracks opened and two hundred fell down to death. With his third snort cracks opened, Enkidu doubled over but instantly recovered, he dodged aside and leapt on the Bull and seized it by the horns. The Bull of Heaven foamed in his face, it brushed him with the thick of its tail. Enkidu cried to Gilgamesh, 'My friend, we boasted that we would leave enduring names behind us. Now thrust in your sword between the nape and the horns.' So Gilgamesh followed the Bull, he seized the thick of its tail, he thrust the sword between the nape and the horns and slew the Bull. When they had killed the Bull of Heaven they cut out its heart and gave it to Shamash, and the brothers rested.

But Ishtar rose up and mounted the great wall of Uruk; she sprang on to the tower and uttered a curse: 'Woe to Gilgamesh, for he has scorned me in killing the Bull of Heaven.' When Enkidu heard these words he tore out the Bull's right thigh and tossed it in her face saying, 'If I could lay my hands on you, it is this I should do to you, and lash the entrails to your side.' Then Ishtar called together her people, the dancing and singing girls, the prostitutes of the temple, the courtesans. Over the thigh of the Bull of Heaven she set up lamentation.

But Gilgamesh called the smiths and the armourers, all of them together. They admired the immensity of the horns. They were plated with lapis lazuli two fingers thick. They were thirty pounds each in weight, and their capacity in oil was six measures, which he gave to his guardian god, Lugulbanda. But he carried the horns into the palace and hung them on the wall. Then they washed their hands in Euphrates, they embraced each other and went away. They drove through the streets of Uruk where the heroes were gathered to see them, and Gilgamesh called to the singing girls, 'Who is most glorious of the heroes, who is most eminent among men?' 'Gilgamesh is the most glorious of heroes, Gilgamesh is most eminent among men.' And now there was feasting, and celebrations and joy in the palace, till the heroes lay down saying, 'Now we will rest for the night.'

When the daylight came Enkidu got up and cried to Gilgamesh, 'O my brother, such a dream I had last night. Anu, Enlil, Ea and heavenly Shamash took counsel together, and Anu said to Enlil, "Because they have killed the Bull of Heaven, and because they have killed Humbaba who guarded the Cedar Mountain one of the two must die." Then glorious Shamash answered the hero Enlil, "It was by your command they killed the Bull of Heaven, and killed Humbaba, and must Enkidu die although innocent?" Enlil flung round in rage at glorious Shamash, "You dare to say this, you who went about with them every day like one of themselves!"'

So Enkidu lay stretched out before Gilgamesh; his tears ran down in streams and he said to Gilgamesh, 'O my brother, so dear as you are to me, brother, yet they will take me from you.' Again he said, 'I must sit down on the threshold of the dead and never again will I see my dear brother with my eyes.'

While Enkidu lay alone in his sickness he cursed the gate as though it was living flesh, 'You there, wood of the gate, dull and insensible, witless, I searched for you over twenty leagues until I saw the towering cedar. There is no wood like you in our land. Seventy-two cubits high and twenty-four wide, the pivot and the ferrule and the jambs are perfect. A master craftsman from Nippur has made you; but O, if I had known the conclusion! If I had known that this was all the good that would come of it, I would have raised the axe and split you into little pieces and set up here a gate of wattle instead. Ah, if only some future king had brought you here, or some god had fashioned you. Let him obliterate my name and write his own, and the curse fall on him instead of on Enkidu.'

With the first brightening of dawn Enkidu raised his head and wept before the Sun God, in the brilliance of the sunlight his tears streamed down. 'Sun God, I beseech you, about that vile Trapper, that Trapper of nothing because of whom I was to catch less than my comrade; let him catch least, make his game scarce, make him feeble, taking the smaller of every share, let his quarry escape from his nets.'

When he had cursed the Trapper to his heart's content he turned on the harlot. He was roused to curse her also. 'As for you, woman, with a great curse I curse you! I will promise you a destiny to all eternity. My curse shall come on you soon and sudden. You shall be without a roof for your commerce, for you shall not keep house with other girls in the tavern, but do your business in places fouled by the vomit of the drunkard. Your hire will be potter's earth, your thievings will be flung into the hovel, you will sit at the cross-roads in the dust of the potter's quarter, you will make your bed on the dunghill at night, and by day take your stand in the wall's shadow. Brambles and thorns will tear your feet, the drunk and the dry will strike your cheek and your mouth will ache. Let you be stripped of your purple dyes, for I too once in the wilderness with my wife had all the treasure I wished.'

When Shamash heard the words of Enkidu he called to him from heaven: 'Enkidu, why are you cursing the woman, the mistress who taught you to eat bread fit for gods and drink wine of kings? She who put upon you a magnificent garment, did she not give you glorious Gilgamesh for your companion, and has not Gilgamesh, your own brother, made you rest on a royal bed and recline on a couch at his left hand? He has made the princes of the earth kiss your feet, and now all the people of Uruk lament and wail over you. When you are dead he will let his hair grow long for your sake, he will wear a lion's pelt and wander through the desert.'

When Enkidu heard glorious Shamash his angry heart grew quiet, he called back the curse and said, 'Woman, I promise you another destiny. The mouth which cursed you shall bless you! Kings, princes and nobles shall adore you. On your account a man though twelve miles off will clap his hand to his thigh and his hair will twitch. For you he will undo his belt and open his treasure and you shall have your desire; lapis lazuli, gold and carnelian from the heap in the treasury. A ring for your hand and a robe shall be yours. The priest will lead you into the presence of the gods. On your account a wife, a mother of seven, was forsaken.'

As Enkidu slept alone in his sickness, in bitterness of spirit he poured out his heart to his friend. 'It was I who cut down the cedar, I who levelled the forest, I who slew Humbaba and now see what has become of me. Listen, my friend, this is the dream I dreamed last night. The heavens roared, and earth rumbled back an answer; between them stood I before an awful being, the sombre-faced man-bird; he had directed on me his purpose. His was a vampire face, his foot was a lion's foot, his hand was an eagle's talon. He fell on me and his claws were in my hair, he held me fast and I smothered; then he transformed me so that my arms became wings covered with feathers. He turned his stare towards me, and he led me away to the palace of Irkalla, the Queen of Darkness, to the house from which none who enters ever returns, down the road from which there is no coming back.

'There is the house whose people sit in darkness; dust is their food and clay their meat. They are clothed like birds with wings for covering, they see no light, they sit in darkness. I entered the house of dust and I saw the kings of the earth, their crowns put away for ever; rulers and princes, all those who once wore kingly crowns and ruled the world in the days of old. They who had stood in the place of the gods like Anu and Enlil, stood now like servants to fetch baked meats in the house of dust, to carry cooked meat and cold water from the water-skin. In the house of dust which I entered were high priests and acolytes, priests of the incantation and of ecstasy; there were servers of the temple, and there was Etana, that king of Kish whom the eagle carried to heaven in the days of old. I saw also Samuqan, god of cattle, and there was Ereshkigal the Queen of the Underworld; and Belit-Sheri squatted in front of her, she who is recorder of the gods and keeps the book of death. She held a tablet from which she read. She raised her head, she saw me and spoke: "Who has brought this one here?" Then I awoke like a man drained of blood who wanders alone in a waste of rushes; like one whom the bailiff has seized and his heart pounds with terror.'

Gilgamesh had peeled off his clothes, he listened to his words and wept quick tears, Gilgamesh listened and his tears flowed. He opened his mouth and spoke to Enkidu: 'Who is there in strong-walled Uruk who has wisdom like this? Strange things have been spoken, why does your heart speak strangely? The dream was marvellous but the terror was great; we must treasure the dream whatever the terror; for the dream has shown that misery comes at last to the healthy man, the end of life is sorrow.' And Gilgamesh lamented, 'Now I will pray to the great gods, for my friend had an ominous dream.'

This day on which Enkidu dreamed came to an end and he lay stricken with sickness. One whole day he lay on his bed and his suffering increased. He said to Gilgamesh, the friend on whose account he had left the wilderness, 'Once I ran for you, for the water of life, and I now have nothing.' A second day he lay on his bed and Gilgamesh watched over him but the sickness increased. A third day he lay on his bed, he called out to Gilgamesh, rousing him up. Now he was weak and his eyes were blind with weeping. Ten days he lay and his suffering increased, eleven and twelve days he lay on his bed of pain. Then he called to Gilgamesh, 'My friend, the great goddess cursed me and I must die in shame. I shall not die like a man fallen in battle; I feared to fall, but happy is the man who falls in the battle, for I must die in shame.' And Gilgamesh wept over Enkidu. With the first light of dawn he raised his voice and said to the counsellors of Uruk:

'Hear me, great ones of Uruk,
I weep for Enkidu, my friend,
Bitterly moaning like a woman mourning
I weep for my brother.
O Enkidu, my brother,
You were the axe at my side,
My hand's strength, the sword in my belt,
The shield before me,
A glorious robe, my fairest ornament;
An evil Fate has robbed me.
The wild ass and the gazelle
That were father and mother,
All long-tailed creatures that nourished you
Weep for you,
All the wild things of the plain and pastures;
The paths that you loved in the forest of cedars
Night and day murmur.
Let the great ones of strong-walled Uruk
Weep for you;
Let the finger of blessing
Be stretched out in mourning;
Enkidu, young brother. Hark,
There is an echo through all the country
Like a mother mourning.
Weep all the paths where we walked together;
And the beasts we hunted, the bear and hyena,
Tiger and panther, leopard and lion,
The stag and the ibex, the bull and the doe.
The river along whose banks we used to walk,
 Weeps for you,
Ula of Elam and dear Euphrates
Where once we drew water for the water-skins.
The mountain we climbed where we slew the Watchman,
Weeps for you.

The warriors of strong-walled Uruk
Where the Bull of Heaven was killed,
Weep for you.
All the people of Eridu
Weep for you Enkidu.
Those who brought grain for your eating
Mourn for you now;
Who rubbed oil on your back
Mourn for you now;
Who poured beer for your drinking
Mourn for you now.
The harlot who anointed you with fragrant ointment
Laments for you now;
The women of the palace, who brought you a wife,
A chosen ring of good advice,
Lament for you now.
And the young men your brothers
As though they were women
Go long-haired in mourning.
What is this sleep which holds you now?
You are lost in the dark and cannot hear me.'

He touched his heart but it did not beat, nor did he lift his eyes again. When Gilgamesh touched his heart it did not beat. So Gilgamesh laid a veil, as one veils the bride, over his friend. He began to rage like a lion, like a lioness robbed of her whelps. This way and that he paced round the bed, he tore out his hair and strewed it around. He dragged off his splendid robes and flung them down as though they were abominations.

In the first light of dawn Gilgamesh cried out, 'I made you rest on a royal bed, you reclined on a couch at my left hand, the princes of the earth kissed your feet. I will cause all the people of Uruk to weep over you and raise the dirge of the dead. The joyful people will stoop with sorrow; and when you have gone to the earth I will let my hair grow long for your sake, I will wander through the wilderness in the skin of a lion.' The next day also, in the first light, Gilgamesh lamented; seven days and seven nights he wept for Enkidu, until the worm fastened on him. Only then he gave him up to the earth, for the Anunnaki, the judges, had seized him.

Then Gilgamesh issued a proclamation through the land, he summoned them all, the coppersmiths, the goldsmiths, the stone-workers, and commanded them, 'Make a statue of my friend.' The statue was fashioned with a great weight of lapis lazuli for the breast and of gold for the body. A table of hard-wood was set out, and on it a bowl of carnelian filled with honey, and a bowl of lapis lazuli filled with butter. These he exposed and offered to the Sun; and weeping he went away.

4

THE SEARCH FOR EVERLASTING LIFE

BITTERLY Gilgamesh wept for his friend Enkidu; he wandered over the wilderness as a hunter, he roamed over the plains; in his bitterness he cried, 'How can I rest, how can I be at peace? Despair is in my heart. What my brother is now, that shall I be when I am dead. Because I am afraid of death I will go as best I can to find Utnapishtim whom they call the Faraway, for he has entered the assembly of the gods.' So Gilgamesh travelled over the wilderness, he wandered over the grasslands, a long journey, in search of Utnapishtim, whom the gods took after the deluge; and they set him to live in the land of Dilmun, in the garden of the sun; and to him alone of men they gave everlasting life.

At night when he came to the mountain passes Gilgamesh prayed: 'In these mountain passes long ago I saw lions, I was afraid and I lifted my eyes to the moon; I prayed and my prayers went up to the gods, so now, O moon god Sin, protect me.' When he had prayed he lay down to sleep, until he was woken from out of a dream. He saw the lions round him glorying in life; then he took his axe in his hand, he drew his sword from his belt, and he fell upon them like an arrow from the string, and struck and destroyed and scattered them.

So at length Gilgamesh came to Mashu, the great mountains about which he had heard many things, which

THE EPIC OF GILGAMESH

guard the rising and the setting sun. Its twin peaks are as high as the wall of heaven and its paps reach down to the underworld. At its gate the Scorpions stand guard, half man and half dragon; their glory is terrifying, their stare strikes death into men, their shimmering halo sweeps the mountains that guard the rising sun. When Gilgamesh saw them he shielded his eyes for the length of a moment only; then he took courage and approached. When they saw him so undismayed the Man-Scorpion called to his mate, 'This one who comes to us now is flesh of the gods.' The mate of the Man-Scorpion answered, 'Two thirds is god but one third is man.'

Then he called to the man Gilgamesh, he called to the child of the gods: 'Why have you come so great a journey; for what have you travelled so far, crossing the dangerous waters; tell me the reason for your coming?' Gilgamesh answered, 'For Enkidu; I loved him dearly, together we endured all kinds of hardships; on his account I have come, for the common lot of man has taken him. I have wept for him day and night, I would not give up his body for burial, I thought my friend would come back because of my weeping. Since he went, my life is nothing; that is why I have travelled here in search of Utnapishtim my father; for men say he has entered the assembly of the gods, and has found everlasting life. I have a desire to question him concerning the living and the dead.' The Man-Scorpion opened his mouth and said, speaking to Gilgamesh, 'No man born of woman has done what you have asked, no mortal man has gone into the mountain; the length of it is twelve leagues of darkness; in it there is no light, but the heart is oppressed with darkness. From the rising of the sun to the setting of the sun there is no light.' Gilgamesh said, 'Although I should go in sorrow and in pain, with sighing and with weeping, still I must go. Open the gate of the mountain.' And the Man-Scorpion said, 'Go, Gilgamesh, I permit you to pass through the mountain of Mashu and through the high ranges; may your feet carry you safely home. The gate of the mountain is open.'

When Gilgamesh heard this he did as the Man-Scorpion had said, he followed the sun's road to his rising, through the mountain. When he had gone one league the darkness became thick around him, for there was no light, he could see nothing ahead and nothing behind him. After two leagues the darkness was thick and there was no light, he could see nothing ahead and nothing behind him. After three leagues the darkness was thick, and there was no light, he could see nothing ahead and nothing behind him. After four leagues the darkness was thick and there was no light, he could see nothing ahead and nothing behind him. At the end of five leagues the darkness was thick and there was no light, he could see nothing ahead and nothing behind him. At the end of six leagues the darkness was thick and there was no light, he could see nothing ahead and nothing behind him. When he had gone seven leagues the darkness was thick and there was no light, he could see nothing ahead and nothing behind him. When he had gone eight leagues Gilgamesh gave a great cry, for the darkness was thick and he could see nothing ahead and nothing behind him. After nine leagues he felt the north wind on his face, but the darkness was thick and there was no light, he could see nothing ahead and nothing behind him. After ten leagues the end was near. After eleven leagues the dawn light appeared. At the end of twelve leagues the sun streamed out.

There was the garden of the gods; all round him stood bushes bearing gems. Seeing it he went down at once, for there was fruit of carnelian with the vine hanging from it, beautiful to look at; lapis lazuli leaves hung thick with fruit, sweet to see. For thorns and thistles there were haematite and rare stones, agate, and pearls from out of the sea. While Gilgamesh walked in the garden by the edge of the sea Shamash saw him, and he saw that he was dressed in the skins of animals and ate their flesh. He was distressed, and he spoke and said, 'No mortal man has gone this way before, nor will, as long as the winds drive over the sea.' And to Gilgamesh he said, 'You will never find the life for which you are searching.' Gilgamesh said to glorious Shamash, 'Now that I have toiled and strayed so far over the wilderness, am I to sleep, and let the earth cover my head for ever? Let my eyes see the sun until they are dazzled with looking. Although I am no better than a dead man, still let me see the light of the sun.'

Beside the sea she lives, the woman of the vine, the maker of wine; Siduri sits in the garden at the edge of the sea, with the golden bowl and the golden vats that the gods gave her. She is covered with a veil; and where she sits she sees Gilgamesh coming towards her, wearing skins, the flesh of the gods in his body, but despair in his heart, and his face like the face of one who has made a long journey. She looked, and as she scanned the distance she said in her own heart, 'Surely this is some felon; where is he going now?' And she barred her gate against him with the cross-bar and shot home the bolt. But Gilgamesh, hearing the sound of the bolt, threw up his head and lodged his foot in the gate; he called to her, 'Young woman, maker of wine, why do you bolt your door; what did you see that made you bar your gate? I will break in your door and burst in your gate, for I am Gilgamesh who seized and killed the Bull of Heaven, I killed the watchman of the cedar forest, I overthrew Humbaba who lived in the forest, and I killed the lions in the passes of the mountain.'

Then Siduri said to him, 'If you are that Gilgamesh who seized and killed the Bull of Heaven, who killed the watchman of the cedar forest, who overthrew Humbaba that lived in the forest, and killed the lions in the passes of the mountain, why are your cheeks so starved and why is your face so drawn? Why is despair in your heart and your face like the face of one who has made a long journey? Yes, why is your face burned from heat and cold, and why do you come here wandering over the pastures in search of the wind?'

Gilgamesh answered her, 'And why should not my cheeks be starved and my face drawn? Despair is in my heart and my face is the face of one who has made a long journey, it was burned with heat and with cold. Why should I not wander over the pastures in search of the wind? My friend, my younger brother, he who hunted the wild ass of the wilderness and the panther of the plains, my friend, my younger brother who seized and killed the Bull of Heaven and overthrew Humbaba in the cedar forest, my friend who was very dear to me and who endured dangers beside me, Enkidu my brother, whom I loved, the end of mortality has overtaken him. I wept for him seven days and nights till the worm fastened on him. Because of my brother I am afraid of death, because of my brother I stray through the wilderness and cannot rest. But now, young woman, maker of wine, since I have seen your face do not let me see the face of death which I dread so much.'

She answered, 'Gilgamesh, where are you hurrying to? You will never find that life for which you are looking. When the gods created man they allotted to him death, but life they retained in their own keeping. As for you, Gilgamesh, fill your belly with good things; day and night, night and day, dance and be merry, feast and rejoice. Let your clothes be fresh, bathe yourself in water, cherish the little child that holds your hand, and make your wife happy in your embrace; for this too is the lot of man.'

But Gilgamesh said to Siduri, the young woman, 'How can I be silent, how can I rest, when Enkidu whom I love is dust, and I too shall die and be laid in the earth. You live by the sea-shore and look into the heart of it; young woman, tell me now, which is the way to Utnapishtim, the son of Ubara-Tutu? What directions are there for the passage; give me, oh, give me directions. I will cross the Ocean if it is possible; if it is not I will wander still farther in the wilderness.' The wine-maker said to him, 'Gilgamesh, there is no crossing the Ocean; whoever has come, since the days of old, has not been able to pass that sea. The Sun in his glory crosses the Ocean, but who beside Shamash has ever crossed it? The place and the passage are difficult, and the waters of death are deep which flow between. Gilgamesh, how will you cross the Ocean? When you come to the waters of death what will you do? But Gilgamesh, down in the woods you will find Urshanabi, the ferryman of Utnapishtim; with him are the holy things, the things of stone. He is fashioning the serpent prow of the boat. Look at him well, and if it is possible, perhaps you will cross the waters with him; but if it is not possible, then you must go back.'

When Gilgamesh heard this he was seized with anger. He took his axe in his hand, and his dagger from his belt. He crept forward and he fell on them like a javelin. Then he went into the forest and sat down. Urshanabi saw the dagger flash and heard the axe, and he beat his head, for Gilgamesh had shattered the tackle of the boat in his rage. Urshanabi said to him, 'Tell me, what is your name? I am Urshanabi, the ferryman of Utnapishtim the Faraway.' He replied to him, 'Gilgamesh is my name, I am from Uruk, from the house of Anu.' Then Urshanabi said to him, 'Why are your cheeks so starved and your face drawn? Why is despair in your heart and your face like the face of one who has made a long journey; yes, why is your face burned with heat and with cold, and why do you come here wandering over the pastures in search of the wind?'

Gilgamesh said to him, 'Why should not my cheeks be starved and my face drawn? Despair is in my heart, and my face is the face of one who has made a long journey. I was burned with heat and with cold. Why should I not wander over the pastures? My friend, my younger brother who seized and killed the Bull of Heaven, and overthrew Humbaba in the cedar forest, my friend who was very dear to me, and who endured dangers beside me, Enkidu my brother whom I loved, the end of mortality has over-taken him. I wept for him seven days and nights till the worm fastened on him. Because of my brother I am afraid of death, because of my brother I stray through the wilderness. His fate lies heavy upon me. How can I be silent, how can I rest? He is dust and I too shall die and be laid in the earth for ever. I am afraid of death, therefore, Urshanabi, tell me which is the road to Utnapishtim? If it is possible I will cross the waters of death; if not I will wander still farther through the wilderness.'

Urshanabi said to him, 'Gilgamesh, your own hands have prevented you from crossing the Ocean; when you destroyed the tackle of the boat you destroyed its safety.' Then the two of them talked it over and Gilgamesh said, 'Why are you so angry with me, Urshanabi, for you yourself cross the sea by day and night, at all seasons you cross it.' 'Gilgamesh, those things you destroyed, their property is to carry me over the water, to prevent the waters of death from touching me. It was for this reason that I preserved them, but you have destroyed them, and the *urnu* snakes with them. But now, go into the forest, Gilgamesh; with your axe cut poles, one hundred and twenty, cut them sixty cubits long, paint them with bitumen, set on them ferrules and bring them back.'

When Gilgamesh heard this he went into the forest, he cut poles one hundred and twenty; he cut them sixty cubits long, he painted them with bitumen, he set on them ferrules, and he brought them to Urshanabi. Then they boarded the boat, Gilgamesh and Urshanabi together, launching it out on the waves of Ocean. For three days they ran on as it were a journey of a month and fifteen days, and at last Urshanabi brought the boat to the waters of death. Then Urshanabi said to Gilgamesh, 'Press on, take a pole and thrust it in, but do not let your hands touch the waters. Gilgamesh, take a second pole, take a third, take a fourth pole. Now, Gilgamesh, take a fifth, take a sixth and seventh pole. Gilgamesh, take an eighth, and ninth, a tenth pole. Gilgamesh, take an eleventh, take a twelfth pole.' After one hundred and twenty thrusts Gilgamesh had used the last pole. Then he stripped himself, he held up his arms for a mast and his covering for a sail. So Urshanabi the ferryman brought Gilgamesh to Utnapishtim, whom they call the Faraway, who lives in Dilmun at the place of the sun's transit, eastward of the mountain. To him alone of men the gods had given everlasting life.

Now Utnapishtim, where he lay at ease, looked into the distance and he said in his heart, musing to himself, 'Why does the boat sail here without tackle and mast; why are the sacred stones destroyed, and why does the master not sail the boat? That man who comes is none of mine; where I look I see a man whose body is covered with skins of beasts. Who is this who walks up the shore behind Urshanabi, for surely he is no man of mine?' So Utnapishtim looked at him and said, 'What is your name, you who come here wearing the skins of beasts, with your cheeks starved and your face drawn? Where are you hurrying to now? For what reason have you made this great journey, crossing the seas whose passage is difficult? Tell me the reason for your coming.'

He replied, 'Gilgamesh is my name. I am from Uruk, from the house of Anu.' Then Utnapishtim said to him, 'If you are Gilgamesh, why are your cheeks so starved and your face drawn? Why is despair in your heart and your face like the face of one who has made a long journey? Yes, why is your face burned with heat and cold; and why do you come here, wandering over the wilderness in search of the wind?'

Gilgamesh said to him, 'Why should not my cheeks be starved and my face drawn? Despair is in my heart and

my face is the face of one who has made a long journey.
It was burned with heat and with cold. Why should I not
wander over the pastures? My friend, my younger brother
who seized and killed the Bull of Heaven and overthrew
Humbaba in the cedar forest, my friend who was very
dear to me and endured dangers beside me, Enkidu, my
brother whom I loved, the end of mortality has overtaken
him. I wept for him seven days and nights till the worm
fastened on him. Because of my brother I am afraid of
death; because of my brother I stray through the wilder-
ness. His fate lies heavy upon me. How can I be silent, how
can I rest? He is dust and I shall die also and be laid in the
earth for ever.' Again Gilgamesh said, speaking to
Utnapishtim, 'It is to see Utnapishtim whom we call the
Faraway that I have come this journey. For this I have
wandered over the world, I have crossed many difficult
ranges, I have crossed the seas, I have wearied myself with
travelling; my joints are aching, and I have lost acquaint-
ance with sleep which is sweet. My clothes were worn out
before I came to the house of Siduri. I have killed the bear
and hyena, the lion and panther, the tiger, the stag and the
ibex, all sorts of wild game and the small creatures of the
pastures. I ate their flesh and I wore their skins; and that
was how I came to the gate of the young woman, the
maker of wine, who barred her gate of pitch and bitumen
against me. But from her I had news of the journey; so
then I came to Urshanabi the ferryman, and with him I
crossed over the waters of death. Oh, father Utnapishtim,
you who have entered the assembly of the gods, I wish to
question you concerning the living and the dead, how shall
I find the life for which I am searching?'

Utnapishtim said, 'There is no permanence. Do we

build a house to stand for ever, do we seal a contract to hold for all time? Do brothers divide an inheritance to keep for ever, does the flood-time of rivers endure? It is only the nymph of the dragon-fly who sheds her larva and sees the sun in his glory. From the days of old there is no permanence. The sleeping and the dead, how alike they are, they are like a painted death. What is there between the master and the servant when both have fulfilled their doom? When the Anunnaki, the judges, come together, and Mammetun the mother of destinies, together they decree the fates of men. Life and death they allot but the day of death they do not disclose.'

Then Gilgamesh said to Utnapishtim the Faraway, 'I look at you now, Utnapishtim, and your appearance is no different from mine; there is nothing strange in your features. I thought I should find you like a hero prepared for battle, but you lie here taking your ease on your back. Tell me truly, how was it that you came to enter the company of the gods and to possess everlasting life?' Utnapishtim said to Gilgamesh, 'I will reveal to you a mystery, I will tell you a secret of the gods.'

5

THE STORY OF THE FLOOD

'You know the city Shurrupak, it stands on the banks of Euphrates? That city grew old and the gods that were in it were old. There was Anu, lord of the firmament, their father, and warrior Enlil their counsellor, Ninurta the helper, and Ennugi watcher over canals; and with them also was Ea. In those days the world teemed, the people multiplied, the world bellowed like a wild bull, and the great god was aroused by the clamour. Enlil heard the clamour and he said to the gods in council, "The uproar of mankind is intolerable and sleep is no longer possible by reason of the babel." So the gods agreed to exterminate mankind. Enlil did this, but Ea because of his oath warned me in a dream. He whispered their words to my house of reeds, "Reed-house, reed-house! Wall, O wall, hearken reed-house, wall reflect; O man of Shurrupak, son of Ubara-Tutu; tear down your house and build a boat, abandon possessions and look for life, despise worldly goods and save your soul alive. Tear down your house, I say, and build a boat. These are the measurements of the barque as you shall build her: let her beam equal her length, let her deck be roofed like the vault that covers the abyss; then take up into the boat the seed of all living creatures."

'When I had understood I said to my lord, "Behold, what you have commanded I will honour and perform,

but how shall I answer the people, the city, the elders?"
Then Ea opened his mouth and said to me, his servant,
"Tell them this: I have learnt that Enlil is wrathful
against me, I dare no longer walk in his land nor live in
his city; I will go down to the Gulf to dwell with Ea
my lord. But on you he will rain down abundance,
rare fish and shy wild-fowl, a rich harvest-tide. In the
evening the rider of the storm will bring you wheat in
torrents."

'In the first light of dawn all my household gathered
round me, the children brought pitch and the men what-
ever was necessary. On the fifth day I laid the keel and the
ribs, then I made fast the planking. The ground-space was
one acre, each side of the deck measured one hundred and
twenty cubits, making a square. I built six decks below,
seven in all, I divided them into nine sections with bulk-
heads between. I drove in wedges where needed, I saw to
the punt-poles, and laid in supplies. The carriers brought
oil in baskets, I poured pitch into the furnace and asphalt
and oil; more oil was consumed in caulking, and more
again the master of the boat took into his stores. I slaugh-
tered bullocks for the people and every day I killed sheep.
I gave the shipwrights wine to drink as though it were
river water, raw wine and red wine and oil and white
wine. There was feasting then as there is at the time of the
New Year's festival; I myself anointed my head. On the
seventh day the boat was complete.

'Then was the launching full of difficulty; there was
shifting of ballast above and below till two thirds was
submerged. I loaded into her all that I had of gold and of
living things, my family, my kin, the beast of the field
both wild and tame, and all the craftsmen. I sent them on

board, for the time that Shamash had ordained was already fulfilled when he said, "In the evening, when the rider of the storm sends down the destroying rain, enter the boat and batten her down." The time was fulfilled, the evening came, the rider of the storm sent down the rain. I looked out at the weather and it was terrible, so I too boarded the boat and battened her down. All was now complete, the battening and the caulking; so I handed the tiller to Puzur-Amurri the steersman, with the navigation and the care of the whole boat.

'With the first light of dawn a black cloud came from the horizon; it thundered within where Adad, lord of the storm was riding. In front over hill and plain Shullat and Hanish, heralds of the storm, led on. Then the gods of the abyss rose up; Nergal pulled out the dams of the nether waters, Ninurta the war-lord threw down the dykes, and the seven judges of hell, the Annunaki, raised their torches, lighting the land with their livid flame. A stupor of despair went up to heaven when the god of the storm turned daylight to darkness, when he smashed the land like a cup. One whole day the tempest raged, gathering fury as it went, it poured over the people like the tides of battle; a man could not see his brother nor the people be seen from heaven. Even the gods were terrified at the flood, they fled to the highest heaven, the firmament of Anu; they crouched against the walls, cowering like curs. Then Ishtar the sweet-voiced Queen of Heaven cried out like a woman in travail: "Alas the days of old are turned to dust because I commanded evil; why did I command this evil in the council of all the gods? I commanded wars to destroy the people, but are they not my people, for I brought them forth? Now like the spawn of fish they float in the ocean."

The great gods of heaven and of hell wept, they covered their mouths.

'For six days and six nights the winds blew, torrent and tempest and flood overwhelmed the world, tempest and flood raged together like warring hosts. When the seventh day dawned the storm from the south subsided, the sea grew calm, the flood was stilled; I looked at the face of the world and there was silence, all mankind was turned to clay. The surface of the sea stretched as flat as a roof-top; I opened a hatch and the light fell on my face. Then I bowed low, I sat down and I wept, the tears streamed down my face, for on every side was the waste of water. I looked for land in vain, but fourteen leagues distant there appeared a mountain, and there the boat grounded; on the mountain of Nisir the boat held fast, she held fast and did not budge. One day she held, and a second day on the mountain of Nisir she held fast and did not budge. A third day, and a fourth day she held fast on the mountain and did not budge; a fifth day and a sixth day she held fast on the mountain. When the seventh day dawned I loosed a dove and let her go. She flew away, but finding no resting-place she returned. Then I loosed a swallow, and she flew away but finding no resting-place she returned. I loosed a raven, she saw that the waters had retreated, she ate, she flew around, she cawed, and she did not come back. Then I threw everything open to the four winds, I made a sacrifice and poured out a libation on the mountain top. Seven and again seven cauldrons I set up on their stands, I heaped up wood and cane and cedar and myrtle. When the gods smelled the sweet savour, they gathered like flies over the sacrifice. Then, at last, Ishtar also came, she lifted her necklace with the jewels of heaven that once Anu had

made to please her. "O you gods here present, by the
lapis lazuli round my neck I shall remember these days as
I remember the jewels of my throat; these last days I shall
not forget. Let all the gods gather round the sacrifice,
except Enlil. He shall not approach this offering, for
without reflection he brought the flood; he consigned my
people to destruction."

'When Enlil had come, when he saw the boat, he was
wrath and swelled with anger at the gods, the host of
heaven, "Has any of these mortals escaped? Not one was
to have survived the destruction." Then the god of the
wells and canals Ninurta opened his mouth and said to the
warrior Enlil, "Who is there of the gods that can devise
without Ea? It is Ea alone who knows all things." Then
Ea opened his mouth and spoke to warrior Enlil, "Wisest
of gods, hero Enlil, how could you so senselessly bring
down the flood?

> Lay upon the sinner his sin,
> Lay upon the transgressor his transgression,
> Punish him a little when he breaks loose,
> Do not drive him too hard or he perishes;
> Would that a lion had ravaged mankind
> Rather than the flood,
> Would that a wolf had ravaged mankind
> Rather than the flood,
> Would that famine had wasted the world
> Rather than the flood,
> Would that pestilence had wasted mankind
> Rather than the flood.

It was not I that revealed the secret of the gods; the wise

man learned it in a dream. Now take your counsel what shall be done with him."

'Then Enlil went up into the boat, he took me by the hand and my wife and made us enter the boat and kneel down on either side, he standing between us. He touched our foreheads to bless us saying, "In time past Utnapishtim was a mortal man; henceforth he and his wife shall live in the distance at the mouth of the rivers." Thus it was that the gods took me and placed me here to live in the distance, at the mouth of the rivers.'

6

THE RETURN

UTNAPISHTIM said, 'As for you, Gilgamesh, who will assemble the gods for your sake, so that you may find that life for which you are searching? But if you wish, come and put it to the test: only prevail against sleep for six days and seven nights.' But while Gilgamesh sat there resting on his haunches, a mist of sleep like soft wool teased from the fleece drifted over him, and Utnapishtim said to his wife, 'Look at him now, the strong man who would have everlasting life, even now the mists of sleep are drifting over him.' His wife replied, 'Touch the man to wake him, so that he may return to his own land in peace, going back through the gate by which he came.' Utnapishtim said to his wife, 'All men are deceivers, even you he will attempt to deceive; therefore bake loaves of bread, each day one loaf, and put it beside his head; and make a mark on the wall to number the days he has slept.'

So she baked loaves of bread, each day one loaf, and put it beside his head, and she marked on the wall the days that he slept; and there came a day when the first loaf was hard, the second loaf was like leather, the third was soggy, the crust of the fourth had mould, the fifth was mildewed, the sixth was fresh, and the seventh was still on the embers. Then Utnapishtim touched him and he woke. Gilgamesh said to Utnapishtim the Faraway, 'I hardly slept when you touched and roused me.' But Utnapishtim said,

'Count these loaves and learn how many days you slept, for your first is hard, your second like leather, your third is soggy, the crust of your fourth has mould, your fifth is mildewed, your sixth is fresh and your seventh was still over the glowing embers when I touched and woke you.' Gilgamesh said, 'What shall I do, O Utnapishtim, where shall I go? Already the thief in the night has hold of my limbs, death inhabits my room; wherever my foot rests, there I find death.'

Then Utnapishtim spoke to Urshanabi the ferryman: 'Woe to you Urshanabi, now and for ever more you have become hateful to this harbourage; it is not for you, nor for you are the crossings of this sea. Go now, banished from the shore. But this man before whom you walked, bringing him here, whose body is covered with foulness and the grace of whose limbs has been spoiled by wild skins, take him to the washing-place. There he shall wash his long hair clean as snow in the water, he shall throw off his skins and let the sea carry them away, and the beauty of his body shall be shown, the fillet on his forehead shall be renewed, and he shall be given clothes to cover his nakedness. Till he reaches his own city and his journey is accomplished, these clothes will show no sign of age, they will wear like a new garment.' So Urshanabi took Gilgamesh and led him to the washing-place, he washed his long hair as clean as snow in the water, he threw off his skins, which the sea carried away, and showed the beauty of his body. He renewed the fillet on his forehead, and to cover his nakedness gave him clothes which would show no sign of age, but would wear like a new garment till he reached his own city, and his journey was accomplished.

Then Gilgamesh and Urshanabi launched the boat on to the water and boarded it, and they made ready to sail away; but the wife of Utnapishtim the Faraway said to him, 'Gilgamesh came here wearied out, he is worn out; what will you give him to carry him back to his own country?' So Utnapishtim spoke, and Gilgamesh took a pole and brought the boat in to the bank. 'Gilgamesh, you came here a man wearied out, you have worn yourself out; what shall I give you to carry you back to your own country? Gilgamesh, I shall reveal a secret thing, it is a mystery of the gods that I am telling you. There is a plant that grows under the water, it has a prickle like a thorn, like a rose; it will wound your hands, but if you succeed in taking it, then your hands will hold that which restores his lost youth to a man.'

When Gilgamesh heard this he opened the sluices so that a sweet-water current might carry him out to the deepest channel; he tied heavy stones to his feet and they dragged him down to the water-bed. There he saw the plant growing; although it pricked him he took it in his hands; then he cut the heavy stones from his feet, and the sea carried him and threw him on to the shore. Gilgamesh said to Urshanabi the ferryman, 'Come here, and see this marvellous plant. By its virtue a man may win back all his former strength. I will take it to Uruk of the strong walls; there I will give it to the old men to eat. Its name shall be "The Old Men Are Young Again"; and at last I shall eat it myself and have back all my lost youth.' So Gilgamesh returned by the gate through which he had come, Gilgamesh and Urshanabi went together. They travelled their twenty leagues and then they broke their fast; after thirty leagues they stopped for the night.

Gilgamesh saw a well of cool water and he went down and bathed; but deep in the pool there was lying a serpent, and the serpent sensed the sweetness of the flower. It rose out of the water and snatched it away, and immediately it sloughed its skin and returned to the well. Then Gilgamesh sat down and wept, the tears ran down his face, and he took the hand of Urshanabi; 'O Urshanabi, was it for this that I toiled with my hands, is it for this I have wrung out my heart's blood? For myself I have gained nothing; not I, but the beast of the earth has joy of it now. Already the stream has carried it twenty leagues back to the channels where I found it. I found a sign and now I have lost it. Let us leave the boat on the bank and go.'

After twenty leagues they broke their fast, after thirty leagues they stopped for the night; in three days they had walked as much as a journey of a month and fifteen days. When the journey was accomplished they arrived at Uruk, the strong-walled city. Gilgamesh spoke to him, to Urshanabi the ferryman, 'Urshanabi, climb up on to the wall of Uruk, inspect its foundation terrace, and examine well the brickwork; see if it is not of burnt bricks; and did not the seven wise men lay these foundations? One third of the whole is city, one third is garden, and one third is field, with the precinct of the goddess Ishtar. These parts and the precinct are all Uruk.'

This too was the work of Gilgamesh, the king, who knew the countries of the world. He was wise, he saw mysteries and knew secret things, he brought us a tale of the days before the flood. He went a long journey, was weary, worn out with labour, and returning engraved on a stone the whole story.

7

THE DEATH OF GILGAMESH

THE destiny was fulfilled which the father of the gods, Enlil of the mountain, had decreed for Gilgamesh: 'In nether-earth the darkness will show him a light: of mankind, all that are known, none will leave a monument for generations to come to compare with his. The heroes, the wise men, like the new moon have their waxing and waning. Men will say, "Who has ever ruled with might and with power like him?" As in the dark month, the month of shadows, so without him there is no light. O Gilgamesh, this was the meaning of your dream. You were given the kingship, such was your destiny, everlasting life was not your destiny. Because of this do not be sad at heart, do not be grieved or oppressed; he has given you power to bind and to loose, to be the darkness and the light of mankind. He has given unexampled supremacy over the people, victory in battle from which no fugitive returns, in forays and assaults from which there is no going back. But do not abuse this power, deal justly with your servants in the palace, deal justly before the face of the Sun.'

The king has laid himself down and will not rise again,
The Lord of Kullab will not rise again;
He overcame evil, he will not come again;
Though he was strong of arm he will not rise again;

He had wisdom and a comely face, he will not come again;
He is gone into the mountain, he will not come again;

On the bed of fate he lies, he will not rise again,
From the couch of many colours he will not come again.

The people of the city, great and small, are not silent; they lift up the lament, all men of flesh and blood lift up the lament. Fate has spoken; like a hooked fish he lies stretched on the bed, like a gazelle that is caught in a noose. Inhuman Namtar is heavy upon him, Namtar that has neither hand nor foot, that drinks no water and eats no meat.

For Gilgamesh, son of Ninsun, they weighed out their offerings; his dear wife, his son, his concubine, his musicians, his jester, and all his household; his servants, his stewards, all who lived in the palace weighed out their offerings for Gilgamesh the son of Ninsun, the heart of Uruk. They weighed out their offerings to Ereshkigal, the Queen of Death, and to all the gods of the dead. To Namtar, who is fate, they weighed out the offering. Bread for Neti the Keeper of the Gate, bread for Ningizzida the god of the serpent, the lord of the Tree of Life; for Dumuzi also, the young shepherd, for Enki and Ninki, for Endukugga and Nindukugga, for Enmul and Ninmul, all the ancestral gods, forbears of Enlil. A feast for Shulpae the god of feasting. For Samuqan, god of the herds, for the mother Ninhursag, and the gods of creation in the place of creation, for the host of heaven, priest and priestess weighed out the offering of the dead.

Gilgamesh, the son of Ninsun, lies in the tomb. At the place of offerings he weighed the bread-offering, at the place of libation he poured out the wine. In those days the lord Gilgamesh departed, the son of Ninsun, the king, peerless, without an equal among men, who did not neglect Enlil his master. O Gilgamesh, lord of Kullab, great is thy praise.

GLOSSARY OF NAMES

A SHORT description of the gods and of other persons and places mentioned in the Epic will be found in this Glossary. The gods were credited at different times with a variety of attributes and characteristics, sometimes contradictory; only such as are relevant to the material of the Gilgamesh Epic are given here. The small number of gods and other characters who play a more important part in the story are described in the Introduction; in their case a page reference to this description is given at the end of the Glossary note. Cross-references to other entries in the Glossary are indicated by means of italics.

ADAD: Storm-, rain-, and weather-god.

ANUNNAKI: Usually gods of the underworld, judges of the dead and offspring of *Anu*. See p. 28.

ANSHAN: A district of Elam in south-west Persia; probably the source of supplies of wood for making bows. Gilgamesh has a 'bow of Anshan'.

ANTUM: Wife of *Anu*.

ANU: Sumerian An; father of gods, and god of the firmament, the 'great above'. In the Sumerian cosmogony there was, first of all, the primeval sea, from which was born the cosmic mountain consisting of heaven, 'An', and earth, 'Ki'; they were separated by *Enlil*, then An carried off the heavens, and Enlil the earth. Anu later retreated more and more into the background; he had an important temple in Uruk. See p. 23.

APSU: The Abyss; the primeval waters under the earth; in the later mythology of the *Enuma Elish*, more particularly the sweet water which mingled with the bitter waters of the sea and with a third watery element, perhaps cloud, from which the first gods were engendered. The waters of Apsu were thought of as held immobile underground by the 'spell' of *Ea* in a death-like sleep.

ARURU: A goddess of creation, she created *Enkidu* from clay in the image of *Anu*.

AYA: The dawn, the bride of the Sun God *Shamash*.

GLOSSARY OF NAMES

BELIT-SHERI: Scribe and recorder of the underworld gods.

BULL OF HEAVEN: A personification of drought created by *Anu* for *Ishtar*.

DILMUN: The Sumerian paradise, perhaps the Persian Gulf, sometimes described as 'the place where the sun rises' and 'the Land of the Living'; the scene of a Sumerian creation myth and the place where the deified Sumerian hero of the flood, Ziusudra, was taken by the gods to live for ever. See p. 39.

DUMUZI: The Sumerian form of *Tammuz*; a god of vegetation and fertility, and so of the underworld, also called 'the Shepherd and 'lord of the sheepfolds'. As the companion of *Ningizzida* 'to all eternity' he stands at the gate of heaven. In the Sumerian 'Descent of Inanna' he is the husband of the goddess Inanna, the Sumerian counterpart of *Ishtar*. According to the Sumerian King-List Gilgamesh was descended from 'Dumuzi a shepherd'.

EA: Sumerian Enki; god of the sweet waters, also of wisdom, a patron of arts and one of the creators of mankind, towards whom he is usually well-disposed. The chief god of Eridu, where he had a temple, he lived 'in the deep'; his ancestry is uncertain, but he was probably a child of *Anu*. See p. 26.

EANNA: The temple precinct in Uruk sacred to *Anu* and *Ishtar*.

EGALMAH: The 'Great Palace' in Uruk, the home of the goddess *Ninsun*, the mother of Gilgamesh, See p. 15.

ENDUKUGGA: With *Nindukugga*, Sumerian gods living in the underworld; parents of *Enlil*.

ENKIDU: Moulded by *Aruru*, goddess of creation, out of clay in the image and 'of the essence of *Anu*', the sky-god, and of *Ninurta* the war-god. The companion of Gilgamesh, he is wild or natural man; he was later considered a patron or god of animals and may have been the hero of another cycle. See p. 30.

ENLIL: God of earth, wind, and the universal air, ultimately spirit; the executive of *Anu*. In the Sumerian cosmogony he was born of the union of An heaven, and *Ki* earth. These he separated, and he then carried off earth as his portion. In later times he supplanted *Anu* as chief god. He was the patron of the city of Nippur. See p. 24.

ENMUL: See *Endukugga*.

ENNUGI: God of irrigation and inspector of canals.

ENUMA ELISH: The Semitic creation epic which describes the creation

121

of the gods, the defeat of the powers of chaos by the young god Marduk, and the creation of man from the blood of Kingu, the defeated champion of chaos. The title is taken from the first words of the epic 'When on high'.

ERESHKIGAL: The Queen of the underworld, a counterpart of Persephone; probably once a sky-goddess. In the Sumerian cosmogony she was carried off to the underworld after the separation of heaven and earth. See p. 27.

ETANA: Legendary king of Kish who reigned after the flood; in the epic which bears his name he was carried to heaven on the back of an eagle.

GILGAMESH: The hero of the Epic; son of the goddess *Ninsun* and of a priest of *Kullab*, fifth king of Uruk after the flood, famous as a great builder ai.d as a judge of the dead. A cycle of epic poems has collected round his name. See p. 20.

HANISH: A divine herald of storm and bad weather.

HUMBABA: Also Huwawa; a guardian of the cedar forest who opposes Gilgamesh and is killed by him and *Enkidu*. A nature divinity, perhaps an Anatolian, Elamite, or Syrian god. See p. 32.

IGIGI: Collective name for the great gods of heaven.

IRKALLA: Another name for *Ereshkigal*, the Queen of the underworld.

ISHTAR: Sumerian Inanna; the goddess of love and fertility, also goddess of war, called the Queen of Heaven. She is the daughter of *Anu* and patroness of *Uruk*, where she has a temple. See p. 25.

ISHULLANA: The gardener of Anu, once loved by Ishtar whom he rejected; he was turned by her into a mole or frog.

KI: The earth.

KULLAB: Part of *Uruk*.

LUGULBANDA: Third king of the post-diluvian dynasty of Uruk, a god and shepherd, and hero of a cycle of Sumerian poems; protector of Gilgamesh. See p. 19.

MAGAN: A land to the west of Mesopotamia, sometimes Egypt or Arabia, and sometimes the land of the dead, the underworld.

MAGILUM: Uncertain meaning, perhaps 'the boat of the dead'.

MAMMETUM: Ancestral goddess responsible for destinies.

MAN-SCORPION: Guardian, with a similar female monster, of the mountain into which the sun descends at nightfall. Shown on sealings and ivory inlays as a figure with the upper part of the body human and the lower part ending in a scorpion's tail. According to the *Enuma Elish* created by the primeval waters in order to fight the gods.

MASHU: The word means 'twins' in the Akkadian language. A mountain with twin peaks into which the sun descends at nightfall and from which it returns at dawn. Sometimes thought of as Lebanon and Anti-Lebanon.

NAMTAR: Fate, destiny in its evil aspect; pictured as a demon of the underworld, also a messenger and chief minister of *Ereshkigal*; a bringer of disease and pestilence.

NEDU: See *Neti*.

NERGAL: Underworld god, sometimes the husband of *Ereshkigal*, he is the subject of an Akkadian poem which describes his translation from heaven to the underworld; plague-god.

NETI: The Sumerian form of Nedu, the chief gate-keeper in the underworld.

NINDUKUGGA: With *Endukugga*, parental gods living in the under-world.

NINGAL: Wife of the Moon God and mother of the Sun.

NINGIRSU: An earlier form of *Ninurta*; god of irrigation and fertility, he had a field near Lagash where all sorts of plants flourished; he was the child of a she-goat.

NINGIZZIDA: Also Gizzida; a fertility god, addressed as 'Lord of the Tree of Life'; sometimes he is a serpent with human head, but later he was a god of healing and magic; the companion of *Tammuz*, with whom he stood at the gate of heaven.

NINHURSAG: Sumerian mother-goddess; one of the four principal Sumerian gods with An, *Enlil*, and Enki; sometimes the wife of Enki, she created all vegetation. The name means 'the Mother'; she is also called 'Nintu', lady of birth, and *Ki*, the earth.

NINKI: The 'mother' of *Enlil*, probably a form of Ninhursag.

NINLIL: Goddess of heaven, earth, and air and in one aspect of the underworld; wife of *Enlil* and mother of the Moon; worshipped with Enlil in Nippur.

NINSUN: The mother of Gilgamesh, a minor goddess whose house was in Uruk; she was noted for wisdom, and was the wife of *Lugulbanda*.

NINURTA: The later form of *Ningirsu*; a warrior and god of war, a herald, the south wind, and god of wells and irrigation. According to one poem he once dammed up the bitter waters of the underworld and conquered various monsters.

NISABA: Goddess of grain.

NISIR: Probably means 'Mountain of Salvation'; sometimes identified with the Pir Oman Gudrun range south of the lower Zab, or with the biblical Ararat north of Lake Van.

PUZUR-AMURRI: The steersman of *Utnapishtim* during the flood.

SAMUQAN: God of cattle.

SEVEN SAGES: Wise men who brought civilization to the seven oldest cities of Mesopotamia.

SHAMASH: Sumerian Utu; the sun; for the Sumerians he was principally the judge and law-giver with some fertility attributes. For the Semites he was also a victorious warrior, the god of wisdom, the son of *Sin*, and 'greater than his father'. He was the husband and brother of *Ishtar*. He is represented with the saw with which he cuts decisions. In the poems 'Shamash' may mean the god, or simply the sun. See p. 24.

SHULLAT: A divine herald of storm and of bad weather.

SHULPAE: A god who presided over feasts and feasting.

SHURRUPAK: Modern Fara, eighteen miles north-west of Uruk; one of the oldest cities of Mesopotamia, and one of the five named by the Sumerians as having existed before the flood. The home of the hero of the flood story.

SIDURI: The divine wine-maker and brewer; she lives on the shore of the sea (perhaps the Mediterranean), in the garden of the sun. Her name in the Hurrian language means 'young woman' and she may be a form of *Ishtar*. See p. 38.

SILILI: The mother of the stallion; a divine mare?

SIN: Sumerian Nanna, the moon. The chief Sumerian astral deity, the father of Utu-*Shamash*, the sun, and of *Ishtar*. His parents were *Enlil* and *Ninlil*. His chief temple was in Ur.

TAMMUZ: Sumerian *Dumuzi*; the dying god of vegetation, bewailed by *Ishtar*, the subject of laments and litanies. In an Akkadian poem Ishtar descends to the underworld in search of her young husband Tammuz; but in the Sumerian poem on which this is based it is Inanna herself who is responsible for sending Dumuzi to the underworld because of his pride and as a hostage for her own safe return.

UBARA-TUTU: A king of *Shurrupak* and father of *Utnapishtim*. The
only king of Kish named in the prediluvian King-List, apart from
Utnapishtim.

URSHANABI: Old Babylonian Sursunabu; the boatman of *Utnapish-
tim* who ferries daily across the waters of death which divide the
garden of the sun from the paradise where Utnapishtim lives for
ever (the Sumerian *Dilmun*). By accepting Gilgamesh as a passenger
he forfeits this right, and accompanies Gilgamesh back to Uruk
instead.

URUK: Biblical Erech, modern *Warka*, in southern Babylonia be-
tween Fara (*Shurrupak*) and Ur. Shown by excavation to have been
an important city from very early times, with great temples to the
gods *Anu* and *Ishtar*. Traditionally the enemy of the city of Kish, and
after the flood the seat of a dynasty of kings, among whom Gilga-
mesh was the fifth and most famous.

UTNAPISHTIM: Old Babylonian Utanapishtim, Sumerian Ziusudra;
in the Sumerian poems he is a wise king and priest of *Shurrupak*; in
the Akkadian sources he is a wise citizen of Shurrupak. He is the son
of Ubara-Tutu, and his name is usually translated, 'He Who Saw
Life'. He is the protégé of the god *Ea*, by whose connivance he sur-
vives the flood, with his family and with 'the seed of all living crea-
tures'; afterwards he is taken by the gods to live for ever at 'the
mouth of the rivers' and given the epithet 'Faraway'; or according
to the Sumerians he lives in *Dilmun* where the sun rises.

APPENDIX: SOURCES

THE main sources for this version of the Epic have already been given (see pp. 50–57 ff.). Full bibliographies will be found in *Ancient Near Eastern Texts Relating to the Old Testament*, edited by James B. Pritchard, and *Gilgameš et sa légende*, Cahiers du Groupe François-Thureau-Dangin, and in the *Reallexikon der Assyriologie*; what follows here is a short note on the distribution of the material between the different tablets.

(i) The Sumerian poem 'Gilgamesh and the Land of the Living'; text from fourteen tablets found at Nippur, one at Kish, and two of unknown provenance, giving 175 lines extant. All date from the first half of the second millennium. The following incidents are covered: the friendship of the Lord Gilgamesh and his servant Enkidu, the need to set up a lasting name, entreaty of Utu (Shamash), who appoints supernatural helpers, arming of Gilgamesh and Enkidu, departure with fifty companions, felling of the cedar, Gilgamesh overcome with weakness, dusk on the mountain, dialogue with Enkidu, Huwawa (Humbaba) found in his house, Gilgamesh uproots trees, goes to the house of Huwawa who pleads for his life and is refused on the advice of Enkidu, Huwawa is killed and his body presented to a furious Enlil. Here the Sumerian text breaks off.

(ii) The Sumerian 'Death of Gilgamesh' is still very fragmentary and it is not clear what is its relation to the other Gilgamesh poems, and especially to 'Gilgamesh and the Land of the Living'. The text followed here is taken from the three tablets found at Nippur, dated to the first half of the second millennium. Two fragments, 'A' and 'B', give Enlil's 'Destiny' of Gilgamesh, and the lament for the dead king and account of the funeral offerings; but recently Professor Kramer has identified other fragments which indicate that the 'Death' was inscribed on a tablet with at least 450 lines.

(iii) Old Babylonian versions, dating from the first dynasty of Babylon, first half of the second millennium: the so-called 'Pennsylvania Tablet' gives the coming of Enkidu and the dreams of Gilgamesh concerning him. The 'Yale Tablet' has the preparation for the forest journey up to the departure from Uruk. The 'Meissner' fragment, from Sippar, gives the Siduri episode and the meeting with the ferryman Sursunabu (Urshanabi). An independent publication of the Old Babylonian material was made by M. Jastrow and A. T. Clay in 1920 as *An Old Babylonian Version of the Epic of Gilgamesh*. Recently another Old Babylonian fragment from Tell Iščali has been published by T. Bauer (see now *Ancient Near Eastern Texts referring to the Old Testament*). It deals with the death of Humbaba and does not differ from the Sumerian account so much as do the later Akkadian versions. From the Ur tablets in the British Museum (UET VI), we now have a slightly fuller Middle Babylonian version of Enkidu's sickness: C. J. Gadd, *Iraq*, 28, 1966, 105–21 and Old Babylonian fragments (published by A. R. Millard, *Iraq*, 26, 1964, 99) provide some additions to Tablet IX.

(iv) Hittite version, from tablets found at Boghazköy in central Anatolia, dated to the middle of the second millennium; these contain fragments of the description of Gilgamesh and of his endowments, the forest episode with the felling of the cedar, Enkidu's dream when he is sick and dying, and part of the journey to find Utnapishtim with the Siduri incident and the meeting with Urshanabi. From this point the story appears to diverge widely from other versions. The translation was published by J. Friedrich in the *Zeitschrift für Assyriologie*, 39, 1929, and H. Otten, *Instanbuler Mitteilungen* 8, 1958, 93–125. Another fragment from the Hittite tablets from Boghazköy (KUB VIII, 48, 1924) published now by R. Stefanini, *Journal of Near Eastern Studies*, 28, 1968, gives a slightly different version of the Council of Gods in Enkidu's deathbed dream.

(v) A Hurrian language fragment, also from Boghazköy, gives part of the journey to Utnapishtim. It was published in the *Zeitschrift für Assyriologie*, 35, 1923.

(vi) Semitic versions. An Akkadian version was used in the Hittite Empire and fragments have been found at Boghazköy; but the fullest of all versions is the Assyrian. Originally it was written on twelve tablets of six columns and approximately three hundred lines to each tablet; parts of all twelve still exist. Nearly all are from the palace library at Nineveh, and are seventh century B.C. Based on earlier material, these cover all the incidents of the story up to the return from the search for Utnapishtim. The material is divided as follows: Tablet I, the descriptions of Gilgamesh and of Enkidu up to the end of Gilgamesh's second dream concerning Enkidu. Tablet II, very fragmentary, probably covered the encounter of Gilgamesh and Enkidu and the first mention of the cedar forest. Tablet III, also very fragmentary, probably has Gilgamesh's interviews with the counsellors, with Ninsun, and the commission to Enkidu. Tablet IV, of which only a few lines survive, probably covered the journey to the forest and the arrival at the gate. Tablet V had the description of the forest, the dreams on the mountain, and probably the meeting with and killing of Humbaba. Tablet VI had the encounter of Gilgamesh and Ishtar, the incident of the Bull of Heaven, and the beginning of Enkidu's sickness. Tablet VII had Enkidu's sickness continued, his dreams and death. Tablet VIII had the lament over Enkidu and probably a description of the funeral. Tablet IX covers Gilgamesh's journey to find Utnapishtim up to the meeting with Siduri. Tablet X covers the Siduri incident, Urshanabi, and the finding of Utnapishtim. Tablet XI is the fullest and best preserved of all, with over three hundred extant lines. It describes the Deluge, the testings of Gilgamesh, and his return to Uruk. There is no death of Gilgamesh in the Assyrian recension, and the twelfth and last tablet recounts a separate incident, an alternative to the death of Enkidu as recounted in Tablet VII. Tablet XII is a direct translation from a Sumerian original, which has also survived in part. The relationship between the two has been discussed by Prof. Kramer in the *Journal of the American Oriental Society*, 64, 1944; and by several writers, especially L. Matouš in *Gilgameš et sa légende*.

(vii) The Sultantepe Akkadian fragment. This was excavated by Mr Seton Lloyd and Bay Nuri Gökçe in 1951. Two one-column tablets were found, one a fragment with Enkidu's sickness, and the other with Gilgamesh's lament over Enkidu; and probably also a description of the funeral, and the statue of Enkidu raised by Gilgamesh. Although very short, both fragments fill gaps in the Nineveh recension from which they differ slightly, and Dr Gurney, who has published them in the *Journal of Cuneiform Studies*, 8, 1954, and *Anatolian Studies*, II, 1952, thinks they are schoolboys' work with characteristic mistakes.